LOUISIANA *de* MER

LOUISIANA *de* MER

⚜

seasonal SEAFOOD recipes

hm | books

PRESIDENT/CCO Brian Hart Hoffman
VICE PRESIDENT/EDITORIAL Cindy Smith Cooper
ART DIRECTOR Cailyn Haynes
CONTRIBUTING ART DIRECTOR Amy Merk

LOUISIANA COOKIN' EDITORIAL

EDITORIAL DIRECTOR Brooke Michael Bell
EDITOR Daniel Schumacher
CREATIVE DIRECTOR/PHOTOGRAPHY Mac Jamieson
CREATIVE DIRECTOR/ART Deanna Rippy Gardner
ASSISTANT EDITOR Courtney McDuff
COPY EDITOR Avery Hurt
PHOTO STYLIST Mary Beth Stillwell
CONTRIBUTING PHOTO STYLISTS Anna Pollock Rayner,
Katherine Tucker, Vanessa Rocchio
SENIOR PHOTOGRAPHERS John O'Hagan, Marcy Black Simpson
PHOTOGRAPHERS Jim Bathie, William Dickey, Stephanie Welbourne
EXECUTIVE CHEF Rebecca Treadwell
TEST KITCHEN PROFESSIONALS Allene Arnold, Kathleen Kanen,
Janet Lambert, Anna Theoktisto, Loren Wood
TEST KITCHEN ASSISTANT Anita Simpson Spain
SENIOR DIGITAL IMAGING SPECIALIST Delisa McDaniel
DIGITAL IMAGING SPECIALIST Clark Densmore

hm
hoffmanmedia

CHAIRMAN OF THE BOARD/CEO Phyllis Hoffman DePiano
PRESIDENT/COO Eric W. Hoffman
PRESIDENT/CCO Brian Hart Hoffman
EXECUTIVE VICE PRESIDENT/OPERATIONS & MANUFACTURING Greg Baugh
VICE PRESIDENT/DIGITAL MEDIA Jon Adamson
VICE PRESIDENT/EDITORIAL Cindy Smith Cooper
VICE PRESIDENT/ADMINISTRATION Lynn Lee Terry

Hoffman Media
1900 International Park Drive, Suite 50
Birmingham, Alabama 35243
hoffmanmedia.com

ISBN # 978-1-940772-18-9
Printed in Mexico

Cover recipe on page 148

Contents

Introduction

The fruits of the sea have always been a central focus of Louisiana cooking. From the fertile Gulf of Mexico and the Mighty Mississippi to bayous and inland lakes, local waters provide an abundance of inspiration.

FOR CENTURIES, Louisianians have embraced the natural bounty of their homeland, transforming humble catfish and crawfish into iconic dishes that capture the soul of this place. Whether grilled, stewed, fried, panéed, or otherwise prepared, foods served by chefs and cooks around the Bayou State honor Cajun and Creole traditions and allow us to enjoy the foods of our ancestors.

As the seasons change, so do the varieties of seafood on the table. Crawfish are eaten with abandon during the spring and early summer months, but by June, when they begin burrowing back into the Cajun Country mud, tastes move on to finfish and brown shrimp.

From simply roasted oysters in the fall and winter to decadent Creole creations, this collection contains both traditional and updated recipes that celebrate Louisiana's love of seafood, and will help nourish and delight your family throughout the year.

Local Pantry

CAJUN (OR CREOLE) SEASONING

Because they add a spicy, salty background to dishes, seasoning mixes are a go-to for many Louisiana home cooks. Each commercial variety has its own unique flavor profile, some leaning heavily on cayenne, while others amp up paprika and dried herbs. Since MSG is frequently added to these mixes, we prefer to keep a homemade version on hand to control the salt level (see variations on page 155).

CANE VINEGAR

This mild vinegar made from Louisiana sugarcane adds a smoky flavor to vinaigrettes and glazes. If you can't find Steen's Cane Vinegar, white wine vinegar or cider vinegar are good substitutes.

CAYENNE

Cayenne peppers are a central part of Louisiana cuisine. Always be sure to test the freshness of dried cayenne, as it loses potency over time. If you've had that jar for more than a year, it's probably time for a new one.

CREOLE MUSTARD

Whereas mustard is typically relegated to sandwich condiment status, in Louisiana the spicy zing of Creole mustard can be found in dressings, marinades, and sauces (including the creamy New Orleans rémoulade). Zatarain's is a notable producer.

GRITS

Stone-ground grits are popular throughout the South, and Louisiana is no exception. Some area producers include Louisiana Pride Grist Mill, from Pride, Louisiana, (*louisianapridegristmill.com*) and McEwen & Sons (*mcewenandsons.com*). The quick-cooking cracked jasmine rice (basically rice grits) by Cajun Grain Rice from Kinder, Louisiana, is a terrific local alternative to corn grits (*cajungrain.com*).

FILÉ POWDER

Made from ground sassafras leaves, filé powder acts both as a thickening agent for gumbos and as a spice. It is nationally available from companies including Tony Chachere's, Cajun Chef, and McCormick.

HOT SAUCE

Louisiana-style hot sauce typically uses red peppers, such as tabasco and cayenne, which are salt-brined and fermented. Each commercial hot sauce has its own flavor profile—some fiery hot, others quite salty—so it is important to try a few to see which best suits your taste.

RICE

Farmers across Louisiana—primarily in the southwest, but also in the northeast—plant nearly 400,000 acres of rice each year. Long-grain rice is by far the most common type grown, and cooks should seek out aromatic varieties including pecan rice and popcorn rice (which smell and taste like their namesakes).

PECAN OIL

With a mild flavor and high smoke point, pecan oil is a versatile pantry staple. It is well-suited for salad dressings and a delightful substitute for canola when pan-frying. Kinloch Pecan Oil (*pecanoil.com*) and Inglewood Farm (*inglewoodfarm.com*) are noteworthy.

CARNIVAL TIME

From January 6 through Mardi Gras Day,
we let the good times roll with warming gumbos,
hearty soups, and decadent party dishes.

Shrimp and Tasso Soup *15* | Myrtle Grove Seafood Gumbo *16*

Broiled Oysters *18* | Crawfish and Stone-Ground Grits Gratin *21*

Snapper with Pomelo-Avocado Salsa *23*

Seafood Gumbo *24* | Crawfish and Corn Beignets *27*

Crawfish Dip with Fried Bow Tie Pasta *28*

New Orleans Barbecue Shrimp *31*

Seafood Pasta with Tomato Cream Sauce *32*

Crawfish and Green Onion Bread Pudding *34*

Snapper with Tomatoes and Capers *37*

Shrimp and Tasso Soup

MAKES ABOUT 8 SERVINGS

3 quarts water
2 tablespoons salt, divided
1 lemon, halved
1 bay leaf
1 dried red pepper
3 cups white wine, divided
2 pounds large fresh shrimp
8 ounces tasso ham, finely diced
2 tablespoons olive oil
1½ cups diced onion
1 cup diced carrot
1 cup diced celery
1 cup diced green bell pepper
1 cup diced red bell pepper
¼ cup chopped green onion
3 tablespoons minced jalapeño
2 tablespoons minced garlic
1 tablespoon Cajun seasoning
2 teaspoons ground black pepper
Garnish: fresh parsley

In a large Dutch oven, add 3 quarts water and 1 tablespoon salt. Squeeze juice from lemon into water. Add lemon, bay leaf, dried pepper, and 1½ cups wine. Bring mixture to a boil over high heat. Add shrimp, and cook until shrimp are pink and firm. Remove from heat. Remove shrimp, and drain, reserving liquid. Transfer shrimp to ice water bath to stop the cooking process, and let stand 5 minutes. Peel shrimp, and add shells to reserved cooking liquid, reserving shrimp. Cook liquid over medium-high heat for 20 minutes; strain mixture through a fine-mesh sieve into a large bowl; discard solids.

In same Dutch oven, cook tasso over medium-high heat until browned; let drain on paper towels.

Add oil, and heat over medium-high heat. Add onion, carrot, celery, bell peppers, green onion, jalapeño, and garlic, and cook, stirring often, 3 to 5 minutes or until tender. Add remaining 1½ cups wine and stir, scraping browned bits from bottom of pan. Continue cooking until almost all wine is reduced. Add reserved shrimp broth, remaining 1 tablespoon salt, Cajun seasoning, and pepper. Simmer over medium-high heat for 10 minutes.

Add reserved shrimp and tasso, and simmer 5 minutes. Garnish with parsley, if desired.

Tasso ham, a smoked ham rubbed with pepper and Cajun spices, plays well with sweet Louisiana shrimp in this warming winter soup.

Myrtle Grove Seafood Gumbo

MAKES 10 TO 12 SERVINGS

1½ pounds andouille sausage, sliced
1 pound chicken legs
1 pound chicken wings, tips removed
1 (8-ounce) package chopped ham
4 cups chopped yellow onion
1½ cups chopped green onion
1 cup chopped green bell pepper
1 cup chopped celery
1 tablespoon minced garlic
3 tablespoons vegetable oil
¼ cup all-purpose flour
8 cups water
2 bay leaves
1 to 2 tablespoons crushed red pepper
1 tablespoon Worcestershire sauce
1 tablespoon hot sauce
1 tablespoon filé powder
2 teaspoons kosher salt
3 cooked gumbo crabs, halved
1 pound medium fresh shrimp, peeled and deveined
12 fresh oysters, shucked and drained (reserve oyster liquor)
3 to 4 cups long-grain rice, cooked according to package directions
Garnish: fresh parsley

Heat a large Dutch oven over medium-high heat. Add sausage, and cook until browned; set aside. Add chicken legs and wings, and cook until browned; set aside. Add ham, and cook until browned; set aside.

Add yellow onion, and cook about 10 minutes or until softened. Add green onion, bell pepper, celery, and garlic, and cook, stirring often, about 10 minutes or until softened; set aside.

Reduce heat to medium; add oil, and cook until hot. Add flour, and cook, stirring frequently, until roux is brown. Add 8 cups water. Increase heat to high, and bring mixture to a boil. Reduce heat to low. Add reserved chicken, sausage, ham, and onion mixture. Add bay leaves, red pepper, Worcestershire, hot sauce, filé, and salt. Increase heat to medium, and simmer 30 minutes.

Add crabs, shrimp, and oysters, and cook about 10 minutes or until seafood is cooked through. Serve with rice. Garnish with parsley, if desired.

This seafood-packed gumbo from Aunt Marylue's Creole/Cajun Cooking and More *by W. Je'an combines some of Louisiana's best flavors.*

Broiled Oysters

3   slices thick-cut smoked bacon,
    cut into ¼-inch pieces
3   tablespoons unsalted butter, divided
½   cup finely chopped yellow onion
¼   cup finely chopped red bell pepper
¼   cup finely chopped green bell pepper
2   cloves garlic, minced
½   cup freshly grated Parmesan cheese
¼   cup freshly grated Romano cheese
1   tablespoon chopped fresh parsley
1   tablespoon chopped fresh chives
3   tablespoons fresh lemon juice
1   teaspoon cracked black peppercorns
4   cups rock salt
12 fresh oysters in shell
Garnish: lemon zest

In a large skillet, cook bacon over medium heat until crisp. Remove bacon using a slotted spoon, and let drain on paper towels. Set aside.

In same skillet, melt 1 tablespoon butter over medium heat. Add onion, and cook 3 minutes or until soft and beginning to brown. Add bell peppers, and cook 4 minutes or until soft. Add garlic, and cook 30 seconds or until fragrant. Transfer mixture to a medium bowl, and set aside. To onion mixture, add reserved bacon, cheeses, parsley, chives, lemon juice, pepper, and remaining 2 tablespoons butter; stir to combine. Set aside, or cover, and refrigerate until ready to cook oysters. Mixture can be prepared up to 1 day ahead.

Preheat oven to broil. On a rimmed baking sheet, pour rock salt to a depth of ¼ inch. Scrub oyster shells, and open, discarding tops. Run a knife under meat of oyster to release from shells. Arrange shell bottoms (containing oysters) on prepared pan. Top each oyster with 1 tablespoon reserved onion mixture.

Broil 3 inches from heat for 4 to 5 minutes or until bubbly and beginning to brown. Garnish with lemon zest, if desired. Serve immediately.

In New Orleans, charbroiled oysters, heavy with butter, garlic, and molten Parmesan cheese, are a cool-weather rite—a party in and of themselves.

Crawfish and Stone-Ground Grits Gratin

MAKES 8 SERVINGS

4 cups seafood stock*
1 cup stone-ground grits
2 teaspoons salt, divided
1 teaspoon ground black pepper, divided
8 ounces goat cheese
1 tablespoon canola oil, plus more for coating pan
1 shallot, finely chopped
1 stalk celery, finely chopped
1 small jalapeño, seeded and finely chopped (optional)
2 cloves garlic, finely chopped
1 pound cooked crawfish tails*
¼ cup white wine
4 large eggs, lightly beaten
¼ cup chopped fresh parsley
¼ cup chopped green onion

In a large saucepan, bring seafood stock to a boil over medium-high heat. Slowly whisk in grits, 1 teaspoon salt, and ½ teaspoon pepper. Reduce heat to low, and simmer, stirring often, about 45 minutes or until creamy and thick. Remove from heat, and stir in goat cheese.

Preheat oven to 350°. Grease a 12-inch round baking dish with oil, and set aside.

In a large skillet, heat 1 tablespoon oil over medium heat. Add shallot, celery, jalapeño, and garlic; cook about 3 minutes or until shallot is soft and translucent. Add crawfish or shrimp, wine, and remaining 1 teaspoon salt and ½ teaspoon pepper; cook 4 minutes.

Transfer half of crawfish mixture to a medium bowl, and set side. Add eggs and remaining crawfish mixture to grits; stir to combine. Spoon grits mixture into prepared baking dish. Top with remaining crawfish mixture, parsley, and green onion. Mixture may be covered and refrigerated up to 1 day. Bring to room temperature before baking.

Bake about 45 minutes or until bubbly and golden brown. Let cool slightly before serving.

*1 (8-ounce) bottle clam juice and 3 cups water may be substituted for seafood stock. Small fresh shrimp may be substituted for crawfish tails.

When entertaining during Mardi Gras, cookbook author Virginia Willis delights brunch guests with this delicious make-ahead gratin.

Snapper with Pomelo-Avocado Salsa

MAKES 4 SERVINGS

2   cups coarsely chopped pomelo sections
1   cup chopped avocado
⅓   cup chopped toasted pecans
2   tablespoons finely chopped red onion
2   tablespoons red wine vinegar
1   tablespoon minced jalapeño
¼   teaspoon crushed red pepper
⅓   cup plus 2 tablespoons pecan oil, divided
1¼ teaspoons kosher salt, divided
1   teaspoon ground black pepper
4   (6-ounce) skin-on snapper fillets

In a medium bowl, gently combine pomelo, avocado, pecans, onion, vinegar, jalapeño, red pepper, 2 tablespoons oil, and ¼ teaspoon salt. Set aside.

In a large skillet, heat remaining ⅓ cup oil over medium-high heat. Sprinkle fish with black pepper and remaining 1 teaspoon salt. Gently place 2 fillets in skillet, skin-side down; cook about 3 minutes per side or until golden brown. Repeat with remaining fillets. Serve with pomelo salsa.

Carnival season and citrus season come together in this light, fresh dish. Pomelos are thick-skinned tart fruits that are delightful when cut into sections.

Seafood Gumbo

MAKES 6 TO 8 SERVINGS

1 cup vegetable oil
1 cup all-purpose flour
1½ cups chopped onion
1 cup chopped green bell pepper
1 cup chopped red bell pepper
1 cup chopped celery
3 tablespoons minced garlic
3 cups chopped okra
1½ cups amber beer*
6 cups seafood stock
2 tablespoons filé powder
2 bay leaves
2 teaspoons Cajun seasoning
1 (8-ounce) container crab claw meat, picked free of shell
1 tablespoon Worcestershire sauce
2 tablespoons kosher salt
1½ teaspoons cayenne pepper
1 pound medium fresh shrimp, peeled and deveined
1 pound red snapper fillets, chopped
2 (8-ounce) containers oysters
1 (8-ounce) container jumbo lump crabmeat, picked free of shell
¼ cup chopped fresh parsley
3 cups long-grain rice, cooked according to package directions
Garnish: chopped green onion

In an 8-quart stockpot, heat oil over medium heat for about 5 minutes; whisk in flour until smooth. Cook, whisking frequently, until roux is the color of peanut butter.

Add onion, bell peppers, celery, garlic, and okra. Cook vegetables, stirring often, for 5 minutes. Add beer, stock, filé, bay leaves, Cajun seasoning, crab claw meat, Worcestershire, salt, and cayenne. Bring mixture to a boil; reduce heat to medium, and simmer for about 1 hour.

Add shrimp, fish, oysters, and lump crabmeat to mixture. Cook for 8 to 10 minutes or until seafood is cooked through; add parsley. Serve with rice, and garnish with green onion, if desired.

*We used Abita Amber.

This seafood filé gumbo, chock full of crab, shrimp, oysters, and snapper, is worthy of a special meal.

Crawfish and Corn Beignets

MAKES 8 SERVINGS

4   cups vegetable oil
3   cups all-purpose flour
2   cups whole milk
1   tablespoon baking powder
1   tablespoon Creole seasoning
1   tablespoon minced garlic
1   teaspoon dried thyme
1   teaspoon hot sauce
1   teaspoon salt
1   pound cooked crawfish tails,
    coarsely chopped
1   (15.25-ounce) can corn, drained
¼   cup minced fresh parsley
¼   cup chopped green onion
Rémoulade, for serving

In a large pot, heat oil over medium heat until a deep-fry thermometer registers 350°.

In a large bowl, combine flour, milk, baking powder, Creole seasoning, garlic, thyme, hot sauce, and salt. Add crawfish, corn, parsley, and green onion, stirring to combine.

In batches, carefully drop batter by ¼ cupfuls into oil. Cook until balls float to top of oil; turn and cook 5 minutes more or until browned. Let drain on paper towels, and serve warm with rémoulade.

As people around the Bayou State celebrate Carnival, crawfish season quietly begins. In Lafayette, Louisiana, Chef Patrick Mould serves these savory beignets to hungry revelers.

Crawfish Dip with Fried Bow Tie Pasta

MAKES 6 SERVINGS

FRIED BOW TIE PASTA

Peanut oil, for frying
8   ounces bow tie pasta, cooked according to package directions and drained
⅓   cup yellow cornmeal
3   tablespoons Creole seasoning

DIP

1   cup water
1   (1-ounce) package dried porcini mushrooms
¾   cup unsalted butter
1   bunch green onions, sliced
¼   cup all-purpose flour
2   cloves garlic, chopped
1   pound cooked crawfish tails
2   teaspoons salt
1   teaspoon ground black pepper
½   teaspoon cayenne pepper
2   cups sour cream
1   cup chopped fresh parsley

FOR THE FRIED BOW TIE PASTA
In a large Dutch oven, pour oil to a depth of 2 inches, and heat over medium-high heat until a deep-fry thermometer registers 375°.

Arrange pasta in a single layer over paper towels to remove any remaining water. In a large bowl, combine pasta, cornmeal, and Creole seasoning, tossing well to coat.

Shake excess cornmeal mixture from pasta, and fry in batches 4 minutes or until golden brown. Let drain on paper towels. Pasta will keep up to 1 week in an airtight container.

FOR THE DIP
In a medium microwave-safe bowl, microwave 1 cup water on high or until very hot. Add mushrooms, and let stand 15 minutes or until mushrooms soften. Strain mushrooms through a fine-mesh sieve, reserving liquid. Finely chop mushrooms, and set aside.

In a medium saucepan, melt butter over medium heat. Add green onion, and cook about 3 minutes or until softened. Stir in flour; cook 5 minutes, stirring occasionally. Add mushrooms, reserved mushroom liquid, and garlic; bring to a low boil.

Stir in crawfish tails, salt, and peppers; cook 5 minutes more. Reduce heat to low; stir in sour cream and parsley. Serve warm with Fried Bow Tie Pasta.

Cajun-born writer Amber Wilson often serves this quick-and-easy crawfish dip with fried pasta or pieces of toasted baguette.

One of the most notable things about New Orleans barbecue shrimp is that it isn't grilled. Rather, this decadent Crescent City classic is sautéed in a flavorful butter sauce.

New Orleans Barbecue Shrimp

MAKES ABOUT 4 SERVINGS

2 pounds jumbo or colossal fresh shrimp, heads left on
7 cups cold water
12 tablespoons unsalted butter, divided
2 tablespoons finely chopped fresh rosemary
1½ teaspoons ground black pepper
2 teaspoons Cajun seasoning
2 shallots, minced
4 cloves garlic, minced
¼ cup Worcestershire sauce
¼ cup hot sauce
2 tablespoons fresh lemon juice
½ cup dark or amber beer*
2 loaves French bread, for serving

Peel and devein shrimp, leaving tails on and reserving the heads and shells. Refrigerate shrimp.

In a Dutch oven, add shrimp heads and shells and 7 cups water. Bring to a boil over medium-high heat. Reduce heat to medium, and cook, stirring occasionally, for 15 minutes. Skim any foam as it rises to the surface. Strain through a fine-mesh sieve into a large bowl, and set aside. Reserve 1 cup shrimp stock. Remaining stock can be refrigerated up to 1 week or frozen up to 3 months.

In a large skillet, melt 5 tablespoons butter over high heat. Add rosemary, pepper, Cajun seasoning, shallot, and garlic, and cook, stirring constantly, about 1 minute or until fragrant. Add reserved stock, Worcestershire, hot sauce, and lemon juice. Add shrimp, and cook until pink and firm.

Add beer, and cook 2 to 3 minutes more. Reduce heat to low, and add remaining 7 tablespoons butter. Gently stir until sauce comes together. Serve immediately with French bread.

*We used Abita Amber.

Seafood Pasta with Tomato Cream Sauce

MAKES 12 APPETIZER SERVINGS

3   tablespoons vegetable oil, divided
1½   pounds large fresh shrimp, peeled
     and deveined
1   pound cooked crawfish tails
½   cup chopped yellow onion
2   cloves garlic, minced
2   tablespoons all-purpose flour
2½   cups chopped seeded tomatoes
½   cup chopped fresh basil
1   cup heavy whipping cream
½   cup seafood stock
1   tablespoon tomato paste
1   teaspoon Cajun seasoning
1   cup freshly grated Parmesan cheese
1   (16-ounce) package penne pasta,
     cooked according to package directions

In a large skillet, heat 1 tablespoon oil over medium-high heat. Add shrimp and crawfish; cook 6 to 7 minutes or until shrimp are pink and firm. Remove, and set aside.

Heat remaining 2 tablespoons oil in pan. Add onion and garlic; cook about 4 minutes or until onion is softened. Add flour, and cook 2 minutes, stirring constantly. Stir in tomato and basil, and cook 5 minutes, stirring often.

Add cream, seafood stock, tomato paste, and Cajun seasoning, stirring to combine. Simmer 6 to 7 minutes or until sauce is thickened. Stir in cheese, pasta, and reserved shrimp mixture. Serve immediately.

When cooking for a party at Houmas House
Plantation and Gardens in Darrow, Louisiana, Chef
Jeremy Langlois makes this creamy seafood pasta.

Crawfish and Green Onion Bread Pudding

MAKES 8 TO 10 SERVINGS

2 cups heavy whipping cream
3 large egg yolks
1 large egg
8 cups cubed day-old French bread
   (about 8 ounces)
1 pound cooked crawfish tails
2 cups sliced green onion
2 teaspoons Sriracha sauce
2 teaspoons salt

Spray a 2-quart baking dish with cooking spray.

In a large bowl, whisk together cream, egg yolks, and egg. Add bread, crawfish, green onion, Sriracha, and salt; fold together. Pour into prepared baking dish; let stand at room temperature for 30 minutes, or cover and refrigerate overnight.

Preheat oven to 325°. Bake 1 hour or until center is firm and a knife inserted in the center comes out clean.

While many cooks are familiar with sweet bread puddings,
Chef Mark Falgoust uses Louisiana crawfish tails
to make a savory version that's a perfect winter side dish.

Snapper with Tomatoes and Capers

MAKES 4 SERVINGS

4   (6- to 8-ounce) snapper fillets,
    skin-on and scored
1   teaspoon salt
½   teaspoon ground black pepper
4½ teaspoons olive oil
2   cups arugula
2   tablespoons white wine
Zest and juice of 1 lemon
1   pint grape tomatoes, halved
2   tablespoons capers
2   teaspoons chopped fresh parsley

Season snapper fillets with salt and pepper.

In a large skillet over medium-high heat, add oil. Once oil begins to smoke, add snapper, skin-side down, and cook about 3 minutes or until skin is crisp. Turn fillets, and cook about 2 minutes more or until fillets flake easily when tested with a fork. Transfer fillets to a plate with arugula.

In the same skillet, add wine and lemon zest and juice, and bring to a boil. Add tomatoes. Using the back of a spoon, lightly crush the tomatoes. When liquid has reduced by half, add capers and parsley. Pour over snapper, and serve immediately.

This seared snapper is the best kind of weeknight meal: easy to prepare and full of flavor.

Chef Jared Tees makes the most
of his spring herb garden by topping
grilled shrimp with this bright
and garlicky chimichurri sauce.

Crawfish and Asparagus Alfredo

1   pound asparagus, trimmed and
     cut into 1-inch pieces
12   ounces fettuccine
8   tablespoons butter, divided
½   pound cooked crawfish tails
2   cups freshly grated Parmesan cheese
1   cup heavy whipping cream
¼   cup chopped fresh basil
1   tablespoon chopped fresh oregano
1   teaspoon chopped fresh thyme
½   teaspoon salt
¼   teaspoon ground black pepper
Garnish: grated Parmesan cheese, chopped
     basil, oregano, and thyme

Bring a large pot of salted water to a boil. Add asparagus, and cook about 2 minutes or until tender. Using a slotted spoon, transfer to ice water bath to stop the cooking process; set aside. Add fettuccine to the same pot of boiling water, and cook about 11 minutes or until tender. Drain, reserving ½ cup cooking water.

In a large pot or Dutch oven, melt 6 tablespoons butter over medium heat. Add pasta, and toss to coat. Stir in crawfish and reserved asparagus; cook about 1 minute or until warmed through. Stir in reserved pasta water, cheese, and cream; cook about 2 minutes or until slightly thickened.

Cut remaining 2 tablespoons butter into pats, and stir it in to pasta along with basil, oregano, thyme, salt, and pepper. Toss to combine well. Garnish with additional Parmesan and herbs, if desired. Serve immediately.

The flavor of Louisiana crawfish tails lends itself to creamy, cheesy sauces, and this crawfish pasta is a perennial favorite.

Ultimate Crawfish Boil

MAKES ABOUT 12 SERVINGS

32 pounds live crawfish
3 cups kosher salt
2 Crawfish Boil Packets, divided (page 155)
10 lemons, halved
10 pounds red potatoes, quartered
8 pounds corn on the cob, shucked and halved crosswise
16 heads garlic, halved crosswise
8 pounds andouille sausage, cut crosswise into thirds
Classic Cajun Seasoning (optional, page 155)

Rinse crawfish thoroughly with cold water.

In a large outdoor 60-gallon pot with a crawfish basket, add 1 Crawfish Boil Packet, 3 cups salt, and lemons, squeezing the juices. Fill halfway with water, and bring to a boil over high heat on a heavy-duty outdoor burner.* Add potatoes, corn, and garlic; bring to a boil. Reduce heat, and simmer 15 minutes.

Submerge crawfish and sausage in the water with remaining Crawfish Boil Packet, making sure crawfish are submerged. Return water to a boil. Turn off heat, and cover. Let stand about 30 minutes or until crawfish are tender and float to the top. Serve immediately. Sprinkle with Classic Cajun Seasoning, if desired.

*Follow all safety guidelines according to manufacturer's directions.

While mudbugs are the star of any crawfish boil, we also fill the pot with smoked sausage, corn, and potatoes. Artichokes, halved heads of garlic, and mushrooms are also popular additions.

Crawfish Cornbread

MAKES 8 SERVINGS

1 cup unsalted butter, divided
½ red bell pepper, seeded and chopped
2 green onions, thinly sliced
1 cup cooked crawfish tails
1 tablespoon plus ½ teaspoon salt, divided
¼ teaspoon ground black pepper
¼ teaspoon crushed red pepper
2 cups yellow cornmeal
½ cup all-purpose flour
1 teaspoon baking soda
1 teaspoon baking powder
1¾ cups whole milk
2 tablespoons honey
1 large egg, beaten

Place a 10-inch cast-iron skillet in the oven while oven preheats to 450°.

In a medium skillet, melt ½ cup butter over medium heat. Add bell pepper and green onion, and cook about 5 minutes or until softened. Stir in crawfish, ½ teaspoon salt, and peppers. Set aside.

In a small microwave-safe bowl, place 7 tablespoons butter, and cook on high for about 45 seconds or until melted. Set aside.

In a medium bowl, combine cornmeal, flour, baking soda, baking powder, and remaining 1 tablespoon salt. Stir in milk and honey. Add melted butter and egg, stirring until combined.

Carefully remove skillet from oven; add remaining 1 tablespoon butter, swirling to coat bottom and sides of pan. Pour batter into pan, and bake for 5 minutes. Top batter with crawfish mixture, and bake 10 minutes more or until golden brown. Let cool slightly before serving.

When visiting her family in South Louisiana, writer Amber Wilson often whips up a batch of this crunchy-crust cornbread.

Shrimp, Tomato, and Kale Soup

MAKES 6 TO 8 SERVINGS

1 tablespoon vegetable oil
1 cup chopped onion
1 bulb fennel, trimmed and chopped
6 cloves garlic, minced
1 bunch lacinato kale, tough stems removed and leaves chopped
3 tomatoes, chopped
½ cup dry white wine
¼ cup all-purpose flour
2 (32-ounce) containers vegetable broth
3 (15.5-ounce) cans cannellini beans, drained and rinsed
1 pound extra-large fresh shrimp, peeled and deveined (tails left on)
1 tablespoon chopped fresh rosemary
1 teaspoon kosher salt
1 teaspoon crushed red pepper
½ teaspoon ground black pepper
¼ teaspoon cayenne pepper
3 tablespoons Champagne vinegar
Garnish: fresh parsley

In a large Dutch oven, heat oil over medium heat. Add onion, fennel, and garlic; cook for 5 minutes, stirring occasionally. Add kale and tomatoes; cook 10 minutes or until kale is tender, stirring frequently. Add wine; cook for 2 minutes, stirring occasionally.

Add flour, and cook, stirring constantly, for 2 minutes. Gradually stir in broth and cannellini beans. Bring to a boil over medium-high heat; reduce heat, and simmer for 15 minutes. Add shrimp, rosemary, salt, and peppers; cook 5 to 7 minutes more. Stir in vinegar. Garnish with parsley, if desired.

Throughout Lent—the period between Ash Wednesday and Easter—devout practitioners try to avoid meat. This hearty soup lessens the sacrifice.

Crawfish Bread Bites

MAKES 30 PIECES

1 tablespoon unsalted butter
½ cup chopped onion
1 cup chopped green bell pepper
2 cloves garlic, minced
4 plum tomatoes, seeded and chopped
½ (16-ounce) package cooked crawfish tails
2 cups shredded sharp white Cheddar cheese
1 cup grated Parmesan cheese
1½ teaspoons salt
½ teaspoon ground black pepper
1 loaf French bread, halved lengthwise

Preheat oven to 350°.

In a large skillet, melt butter over medium heat. Add onion, and cook 4 to 6 minutes or until translucent. Add bell pepper, and cook 3 to 5 minutes or until softened. Add garlic, and cook about 1 minute or until fragrant. Remove from heat, and transfer to a large bowl.

To the same bowl, add tomatoes, crawfish, cheeses, salt, and pepper; combine well. Divide crawfish mixture between French bread halves. Bake in oven on a rimmed baking sheet 8 to 10 minutes or until cheese is melted. Slice into pieces, and serve warm.

Inspired by the New Orleans Jazz & Heritage Festival favorite, we made this party-friendly version of cheesy crawfish bread.

Blackened Catfish

1   tablespoon sweet paprika
2½   teaspoons kosher salt
1   teaspoon onion powder
1   teaspoon garlic powder
1   teaspoon cayenne pepper
¾   teaspoon ground white pepper
¾   teaspoon ground black pepper
½   teaspoon dried thyme
½   teaspoon dried oregano
8   (6-ounce) catfish fillets
1   cup melted unsalted butter
Coleslaw (optional)

In a medium bowl, combine paprika, salt, onion powder, garlic powder, peppers, thyme, and oregano. Dredge fish in spice mixture, shaking off excess.

In a large skillet, heat melted butter over medium-high heat. Carefully place fish in pan, and cook 2 to 3 minutes per side or until cooked through. Serve with coleslaw, if desired.

The technique of "blackening" was popularized by Chef Paul Prudhomme. L'Auberge Casino Resort Lake Charles prepares their Blackened Catfish by pan-searing it in butter.

Crawfish and Corn Chowder

MAKES 12 SERVINGS

4 ears yellow corn
½ cup butter
3 tablespoons pecan oil
1 cup chopped yellow onion
½ cup chopped green bell pepper
½ cup chopped celery
1 teaspoon minced garlic
1 pound medium fresh shrimp, peeled and deveined
1 pound cooked crawfish tails
½ cup quick-mixing flour*
3 quarts chicken broth
3 large Yukon gold potatoes, peeled and cut into ¼-inch pieces
1 tablespoon Cajun seasoning
1 teaspoon salt
1 teaspoon cayenne pepper
½ teaspoon ground black pepper
½ teaspoon ground white pepper
½ cup half-and-half
2 green onions, sliced

Cut kernels from corncobs; set aside. In a large bowl, add corncob and run the blunt side of a large knife against the cob, reserving any liquid. Repeat with remaining corncobs, and set aside.

In a large Dutch oven, heat butter and oil over medium-high heat until butter is melted. Add onion, bell pepper, and celery, and cook about 8 minutes or until onion is soft. Add garlic, shrimp, and crawfish; cook, stirring frequently, for 2 minutes.

Add flour, 1 tablespoon at a time, mixing well after each addition. Stir in chicken broth, potato, corn, and corncob liquid. Bring to a boil, and cook for 5 minutes or until slightly thickened. Add Cajun seasoning, salt, and peppers.

Reduce heat, and simmer 30 minutes or until potatoes are soft. Stir in half-and-half; simmer 5 minutes more. Garnish with green onion, if desired.

*We used Wondra quick-mixing flour.

Home entertainer Katie Leithead is known for the cozy kitchen suppers she hosts in Lake Charles. Guests always help themselves to seconds of this savory soup.

Cajun Crab Boil

4   quarts water
2   tablespoons distilled white vinegar
1   Crab Boil Packet (page 155)
4   bay leaves
4   dried chile peppers
3   sprigs fresh thyme
1   head garlic, cloves separated and peeled
¼   cup sea salt
2   lemons, halved
12   fresh crabs
3   pounds new potatoes, scrubbed clean
4   ears corn, shucked and cut crosswise
     into thirds
1   (10-ounce) bag pearl onions, peeled
1   (10-pound) bag ice

In a large stockpot, bring 4 quarts water, vinegar, Crab Boil Packet, bay leaves, chiles, thyme, garlic, salt, and lemons to a boil over high heat. Add crabs, potatoes, corn, and onions. Return mixture to a boil, and cook 5 minutes. Turn heat off, and cover pot for 15 to 20 minutes.

Pour ice into pot. Let crabs stand in water for at least 1 hour before serving. Crabs can be served warm or completely cooled.

Note: 1 (3-ounce) package crab boil in a bag, such as Zatarain's, may be substituted.

When crabs are plentiful,
Cajuns delight in hosting spicy crab boils studded
with ears of corn and new potatoes.

Crawfish Étouffée

MAKES 6 SERVINGS

3   tablespoons canola oil
¼   cup all-purpose flour
6   tablespoons butter
1   large onion, chopped
½   green bell pepper, seeded and chopped
½   yellow bell pepper, seeded and chopped
½   red bell pepper, seeded and chopped
1   stalk celery, chopped
3   cloves garlic, minced
4½   teaspoons salt
4½   teaspoons ground black pepper
½   teaspoon cayenne pepper
½   teaspoon smoked paprika
¼   teaspoon ground thyme
2   (8-ounce) cans tomato sauce
1¾   cups seafood or chicken stock
1   cup half-and-half
1   pound cooked crawfish tails
1   bunch green onions, sliced
1⅓   cups long-grain rice, cooked according to package directions
½   cup finely chopped parsley
Garnish: sliced green onion

In a large Dutch oven, heat oil over medium-high heat; whisk in flour until smooth. Cook, whisking frequently, until roux is the color of chocolate. Add butter and onion, and cook 5 minutes.

Stir in bell peppers, celery, garlic, salt, peppers, paprika, and thyme; cook 7 minutes or until vegetables are softened.

Add tomato sauce and stock; bring to a boil, and cook for 3 minutes or until slightly thickened. Reduce heat; add half-and-half, and simmer 10 minutes.

Stir in crawfish and green onion; cook 5 minutes more or until crawfish is warmed through. Serve over rice, and top with parsley. Garnish with green onion, if desired.

It's often said that a true Cajun can look out at a field of rice and know how much gravy they'd need to smother it. Writer Amber Wilson uses just enough mouthwatering gravy in this traditional étouffée.

Sautéed Spicy Shrimp

MAKES ABOUT 4 SERVINGS

1   pound extra-large fresh shrimp, peeled and deveined (tails left on)
2   teaspoons Extra-Spicy Cajun Seasoning (page 155)
½   cup olive oil
¼   cup vegetable oil

In a 1-gallon resealable plastic bag, combine shrimp, Extra-Spicy Cajun Seasoning, and olive oil. Toss to coat. Refrigerate 8 to 24 hours.

In a medium skillet, heat vegetable oil over medium-high heat. Add shrimp, and cook 1 to 2 minutes per side or until pink and firm.

This simple preparation highlights the variety of Cajun spices and peppers in our Extra-Spicy Cajun Seasoning. For a milder version, use Classic Cajun Seasoning.

Crawfish Macaroni and Cheese

MAKES ABOUT 15 SERVINGS

16 ounces cooked elbow macaroni
2   tablespoons unsalted butter
½   (16-ounce) package cooked
    crawfish tails
1   (8-ounce) jar pimientos, drained
2   cups shredded mozzarella cheese
2   cups shredded sharp Cheddar cheese
1½ cups shredded Parmesan cheese
1   cup shredded Gruyère cheese
1   cup shredded Gouda cheese
1   cup shredded fontina cheese
1   cup whole milk
3   large eggs, beaten
1   teaspoon salt
½   teaspoon ground black pepper
¼   teaspoon garlic powder
⅛   teaspoon cayenne pepper
1   cup crushed buttery round crackers

Preheat oven to 350°. Spray 15 (1-cup) gratin dishes with cooking spray, and set aside.

In a large bowl, combine butter and pasta, stirring until butter melts. Add crawfish, pimiento, cheeses, milk, eggs, salt, pepper, garlic powder, and cayenne.

Divide pasta mixture among prepared dishes, and smooth tops with a spoon. Bake 10 minutes. Top each portion with crushed crackers. Return to oven, and bake about 5 minutes or until edges are bubbly. Serve immediately.

If you don't have individual gratin dishes, bake this cheesy crowd-pleaser in a 4-quart baking dish.

Shrimp Cornbread Muffins

MAKES 12 MUFFINS

2 tablespoons unsalted butter
½ pound large fresh shrimp, peeled and deveined
2 cloves garlic, minced
2¼ teaspoons salt, divided
⅛ teaspoon ground black pepper
2 tablespoons finely chopped chives
1 teaspoon Cajun seasoning
¼ cup all-purpose flour
½ cup yellow corn flour
½ cup yellow cornmeal
2 tablespoons sugar
1 teaspoon baking powder
1 teaspoon baking soda
1 jalapeño, seeded and finely diced
2 large eggs
¾ cup whole buttermilk, well-shaken
2 tablespoons unsalted butter, melted and slightly cooled

Preheat oven to 350°. Spray a 12-cup muffin pan with baking spray with flour.

In a large skillet, melt butter over medium-high heat. Add shrimp, and cook until almost pink and firm; add garlic, ¼ teaspoon salt, and pepper, and cook 1 minute more. Chop shrimp, and place in a bowl. Add chives and Cajun seasoning. Cover, and refrigerate 20 minutes, or up to 2 days.

In a large bowl, whisk together flours, cornmeal, sugar, baking powder, baking soda, jalapeño, and remaining 2 teaspoons salt. In a small bowl, whisk eggs until frothy. Stir in buttermilk and melted butter. Add egg mixture to flour mixture, whisking until just combined.

Divide batter among muffin cups, using about ¼ cup batter per muffin cup. Place 1 tablespoon shrimp mixture in center of each corn muffin. Bake 10 to 12 minutes, and remove from oven. Shrimp mixture should have sunk into the batter. Add 1 tablespoon shrimp mixture to center of each muffin. Return to oven, and bake 2 to 4 minutes or until toothpick inserted into the center comes out clean and edges of muffins are golden brown. Let cool in muffin pan 10 minutes. Carefully remove muffins from pan, and serve immediately.

These pleasantly spiced, upgraded cornbread muffins make an excellent addition to any spring dinner party menu.

An Asian-inspired slaw takes these grilled shrimp po' boys to the next level. If you can't find New Orleans-style French Bread, substitute 10-inch hoagie rolls.

Grilled Crawfish with Spicy Butter

MAKES ABOUT 4 SERVINGS

6 tablespoons kosher salt
4 pounds live crawfish
2 cups butter, softened
2 tablespoons Cajun seasoning

Fill a large pan with water. Add kosher salt, and bring to a boil over high heat. Add crawfish, and cook about 1 minute. Transfer crawfish to ice water bath.

Using a sharp knife, cut crawfish through shell on belly side the entire length. Remove vein, and remove sack behind eyes in head. Rinse crawfish thoroughly, removing any remaining sediment.

In a medium bowl, combine butter and Cajun seasoning. Beat at medium-high speed with a mixer until smooth and creamy. Cover, and refrigerate up to 3 days.

Spray grill basket with nonflammable cooking spray. Preheat grill to medium-high heat (350° to 400°). Place crawfish in grill basket, and grill, shaking basket occasionally, about 6 minutes or until shell turns bright red and meat is cooked through. In a small saucepan, melt butter mixture over medium-high heat. Serve melted butter with crawfish.

If you're looking for an innovative way to serve crawfish to guests during the best weather Louisiana has to offer, grilling those mudbugs is the way to go.

Red Snapper on the Half Shell

MAKES ABOUT 4 SERVINGS

4 (8-ounce) red snapper fillets, skin and scales attached to one side
¼ cup extra-virgin olive oil
1½ teaspoons kosher salt
¾ teaspoon ground black pepper
2 tablespoons fresh lemon zest
4 sprigs fresh thyme
3 cloves garlic, thinly sliced
Garnish: charred lemon slices, fresh thyme

In a large baking dish or roasting pan, place fish skin side down. Drizzle with oil, and sprinkle with salt, pepper, lemon zest, thyme, and garlic. Cover and refrigerate for 2 hours.

Preheat oven to 350°.

Bake for 45 minutes or until fish is done and meat flakes easily. Serve immediately. Garnish with lemon and thyme, if desired.

When he's not in the kitchen, Chef Mark Falgoust loves to be on the water. Cooking red snapper on the half shell—with the skin and scales attached to one side—is one of his favorite preparations.

Roasted Shrimp and Tomato Salad

MAKES 4 SERVINGS

SHALLOT-TARRAGON VINAIGRETTE

¼ cup white wine vinegar
8 teaspoons extra-virgin olive oil
2 tablespoons minced shallot
2 teaspoons whole-grain mustard
1 teaspoon minced fresh tarragon
1 teaspoon honey
½ teaspoon salt
¼ teaspoon ground black pepper

SALAD

¾ pound large fresh shrimp, peeled and deveined
1 cup grape tomatoes
1½ teaspoons olive oil
¼ teaspoon seasoned salt
¼ teaspoon ground black pepper
1 (6-ounce) package baby spinach
¼ cup crumbled feta cheese

Preheat oven to 425°.

FOR THE VINAIGRETTE
In a medium bowl, whisk together vinegar, oil, shallot, mustard, tarragon, honey, salt, and pepper until combined.

FOR THE SALAD
On a large rimmed baking sheet, add shrimp and tomatoes. Add oil, seasoned salt, and pepper; toss to coat. Roast about 10 minutes or until shrimp are pink and firm and tomatoes have burst.

Serve shrimp mixture over spinach topped with Shallot-Tarragon Vinaigrette and feta.

Roasting shrimp is a quick way to bring out their natural sweetness, which also happens to pair quite nicely with this shallot-tarragon dressing.

Grilled Grouper with Deconstructed Salsa

MAKES 6 SERVINGS

6   (6-ounce) grouper fillets
½   cup olive oil
1   teaspoon salt
1   teaspoon ground black pepper
6   cherry tomatoes
6   green onions
2   shallots, quartered
Garnish: fresh dill and fresh parsley

Spray grill rack with nonflammable cooking spray. Preheat grill to medium-high heat (350° to 400°).

Brush fillets with oil, and season with salt and pepper. Grill fish 2 to 4 minutes per side or until opaque and cooked through.

Add tomatoes, green onions, and shallot to grill, and grill until charred. Serve with grouper. Garnish with dill and parsley, if desired.

*Lean and flaky, grouper lends itself to being grilled.
If you can't find grouper, red snapper is a good substitute.*

Grilled Whole Red Snapper

MAKES 4 TO 6 SERVINGS

Zest and juice of 1 lemon
10 sprigs fresh oregano, divided
5   cloves garlic, divided
½   teaspoon crushed red pepper
½   teaspoon kosher salt
½   teaspoon ground black pepper
½   cup pecan oil, plus more for greasing
1   (4- to 6-pound) red snapper, scaled, gills removed, gutted, rinsed, and patted dry
1   lemon, sliced

In the bowl of a food processor, combine lemon zest and juice, leaves from 5 sprigs oregano, 2 cloves garlic, red pepper, salt, and black pepper; pulse to combine. With motor running, slowly pour in oil, and pulse until combined. Set aside.

Score snapper on both sides with parallel slices cutting down to the bone, about two inches apart between the fins and the tail. Fill the fish's cavity with lemon slices, remaining 5 oregano sprigs, and remaining 3 cloves garlic.

Rub herb mixture onto both sides of snapper, being careful of the dorsal fin, which can be very sharp. Cover, and refrigerate 1 to 2 hours.

Rub grill rack with oil. Prepare grill for direct and indirect grilling, and heat to medium-high (350° to 400°). Place snapper over direct heat, and cook 2 to 3 minutes per side or until it begins to char. Carefully move snapper to indirect heat, and cover grill. Grill, covered, 4 to 7 minutes more or until flesh flakes easily. Carefully transfer snapper to a serving platter, and serve immediately.

With only a few simple herbs and spices, red snapper from Baton Rouge writer and radio host Jay D. Ducote is transformed into a work of art.

Grilled Amberjack Po' boy with Macque Choux

MAKES 6 SERVINGS

2   tablespoons unsalted butter
1   (4-ounce) package diced pancetta
2   cups fresh corn kernels (about 4 ears)
½   cup chopped onion
½   cup chopped green bell pepper
¼   cup chopped celery
1   tablespoon chopped fresh thyme
1½   teaspoons salt, divided
4   cloves garlic, minced
3   tomatoes, seeded and diced
½   teaspoon ground black pepper
¼   teaspoon cayenne pepper
6   (7-ounce) amberjack fillets
Olive oil, for brushing fillets
1   tablespoon Cajun seasoning
Rémoulade sauce
2   (16-ounce) baguettes, cut crosswise
      into 3 pieces and split
Garnish: sliced green onion

In a large skillet, heat butter over medium-high heat for 6 to 8 minutes. Reduce heat to medium; add pancetta, corn, onion, bell pepper, celery, thyme, and 1 teaspoon salt. Cook 15 to 20 minutes, stirring often, or until vegetables are tender. Add garlic and tomato, and cook 8 to 10 minutes more. Add remaining ½ teaspoon salt, and peppers. Set aside.

Spray grill rack with nonflammable cooking spray. Preheat grill to medium-high heat (350° to 400°). Brush fillets with oil, and sprinkle with Cajun seasoning.

Grill fish, uncovered, 5 to 6 minutes or until cooked through, turning once.

Spread desired amount of rémoulade on 1 baguette piece. Add 1 fillet, and top with about ⅓ cup corn mixture. Repeat with remaining baguette pieces, rémoulade, corn mixture, and fillets. Garnish with green onion, if desired.

The po' boy, New Orleans's classic French bread sandwich, is always a crowd-pleasing favorite.

Grilled Tuna Salad

MAKES 6 SERVINGS

VINAIGRETTE

¼   cup fresh lemon juice
¼   cup olive oil
1   tablespoon chopped fresh cilantro
1   tablespoon chopped fresh parsley
1   teaspoon salt
½   teaspoon ground black pepper

TUNA SALAD

1½   pounds sushi-grade tuna
      (about 2 inches thick)
3   tablespoons vegetable oil
1½   teaspoons kosher salt
1   teaspoon ground black pepper
1½   cups baby arugula
1   seedless cucumber, peeled
¼   cup thinly sliced radish
1   avocado, sliced

FOR THE VINAIGRETTE
In the container of a blender, combine lemon juice, oil, cilantro, parsley, salt, and pepper; blend 20 to 30 seconds. Use immediately, or cover, and refrigerate up to 1 week.

FOR THE SALAD
Spray grill rack with nonflammable cooking spray. Preheat grill to medium-high heat (350° to 400°). Cut tuna into 2-inch-wide rectangles.

Brush fish with oil to coat. Season fish with salt and pepper, pressing gently to adhere. Grill tuna, turning once, until ⅛-inch border is opaque but still very rare inside. Transfer tuna to cutting board, and cut across the grain into ¼-inch slices. Set aside.

In a medium bowl, combine arugula, cucumber, radish, and avocado. Add 3 tablespoons vinaigrette; toss gently to combine. Divide salad among serving plates. Top salad with tuna. Serve with remaining vinaigrette, if desired.

*A quick blender vinaigrette amps up the flavor
in this colorful tuna salad.*

Crab-Stuffed Shrimp

MAKES ABOUT 6 SERVINGS

2 pounds jumbo or colossal fresh shrimp, peeled and deveined (tails left on)
1 (8-ounce) package crab claw meat, picked free of shell
1 (8-ounce) package jumbo lump crabmeat, picked free of shell
½ cup mayonnaise
⅓ cup butter
½ cup chopped green bell pepper
3 tablespoons chopped shallot
1 tablespoon chopped garlic
2 tablespoons chopped fresh dill
2 tablespoons chopped fresh chives
2 tablespoons chopped fresh parsley
1 large egg, lightly beaten
1½ teaspoons Cajun seasoning
1 teaspoon ground black pepper
1 cup toasted panko (Japanese bread crumbs)
2 (8-ounce) packages prosciutto, cut into 4-inch strips
Creole Beurre Blanc (page 156)

Preheat oven to 375°. Line a rimmed baking sheet with foil. Split shrimp down the back, being careful not to cut all the way through; set aside.

In a medium bowl, combine crab and mayonnaise. In a small saucepan, melt butter over medium-high heat. Add bell pepper, shallot, and garlic. Cook 5 minutes or until tender, stirring occasionally. Remove from heat, and let cool slightly; add to crab mixture along with dill, chives, parsley, egg, Cajun seasoning, pepper, and bread crumbs, stirring to combine.

Spoon about 2 tablespoons crab mixture into cut side of each shrimp. Wrap a strip of prosciutto around crab filling to secure. Place shrimp, seam-side down, onto prepared baking sheet. Bake 20 minutes or until shrimp are pink and prosciutto is browned. Serve warm with Creole Beurre Blanc.

Delicate shrimp and crabmeat are a delight on their own, but paired with salty prosciutto and a crispy panko crust, they are divine.

Grilled Whole Fish

MAKES 4 SERVINGS

---

1   (4-pound) whole fish, cleaned
2   tablespoons lemon zest
1½ teaspoon kosher salt
1   teaspoon ground black pepper
½   cup plus 1 teaspoon extra-virgin
    olive oil, divided
3   cups hickory wood chips, soaked
    in water at least 30 minutes
1   lemon, quartered
Garnish: roasted garlic cloves, grilled
    lemon slices, fresh parsley

With a sharp knife, score each side of fish 3 times, cutting to the bone. Season fish with lemon zest, salt, and pepper. Pour ½ cup oil over fish, and let stand at room temperature for 30 minutes.

Spray grill rack with nonflammable cooking spray. Heat grill to high heat (400° to 450°).

Place fish over the hottest spot on the grill. Close lid, and cook 2 to 3 minutes. Turn fish, and close lid. Cook 5 minutes more. Turn again, moving to a cooler spot on the grill.

Add hickory chips to grill. Close lid, and cook 5 to 6 minutes more or until fish flakes from the bone.

Transfer fish to serving platter. Squeeze lemon quarters over, and drizzle with remaining 1 teaspoon oil. Serve immediately with roasted garlic, grilled lemon, and parsley, if desired.

An avid fisherman, Chef Mark Falgoust often gives larger snappers a turn on the grill with lemon and garlic. To deepen the flavor, he adds a bit of hickory smoke.

Flash-Cured Yellowfin Tuna Rolls

MAKES ABOUT 4 APPETIZER SERVINGS

1½ cups kosher salt
¼ cup ground black pepper
2 tablespoons whole fennel seeds
1 tablespoon sugar
2 tablespoons firmly packed brown sugar
2 tablespoons orange zest
2 tablespoons lemon zest
1 pound sushi-grade yellowfin tuna
½ cup red wine vinegar
½ cup plus 2 tablespoons olive oil, divided
1 teaspoon salt, divided
2 shallots, sliced
½ (12-ounce) jar roasted red peppers, drained
½ teaspoon minced garlic
⅛ teaspoon ground white pepper
4 ounces unsalted goat cheese
1 cup baby arugula
Garnish: alfalfa sprouts

In a medium bowl, combine kosher salt, black pepper, fennel seeds, sugars, and zests. Rub mixture onto tuna, and refrigerate, uncovered, 2 hours. Rinse tuna under cold water, and pat dry with paper towels. Refrigerate tuna, uncovered, 2 hours more.

In a small bowl, combine vinegar, 2 tablespoons oil, and ½ teaspoon salt. Add shallot, and let stand 2 hours.

In the container of a blender, combine red pepper and garlic; process until puréed. While blender is running, slowly add remaining ½ cup oil. Season with remaining ½ teaspoon salt and white pepper. Set aside.

Slice tuna into 10 pieces. To each slice add goat cheese, shallot, and arugula, and roll tuna around filling. Place roasted red pepper coulis on each plate, and top with a tuna roll. Garnish with sprouts, if desired. Serve chilled.

Note: Consuming raw or undercooked seafood may increase your risk of foodborne illness, especially if you have certain medical conditions.

In his kitchen in Lafayette, Louisiana, Chef Jeremy Conner prepares local ingredients with techniques and insights from his career around the United States. These light, fresh tuna rolls are a particular favorite of his.

COMFORT CLASSICS

High energy tailgating parties and grilling sessions abound in the autumn, and dishes like po' boys, soups and gumbos are always welcome.

Crunchy Catfish Tacos with Chipotle Mayonnaise and Apple Slaw

MAKES 4 TO 6 SERVINGS

APPLE SLAW

- 1 (10-ounce) bag angel hair coleslaw mix
- 1 Granny Smith apple, peeled, cored, and finely chopped
- 1 cup thinly sliced carrot
- ½ cup thinly sliced red onion
- 1 jalapeño pepper, seeded and thinly sliced
- ¼ cup fresh lemon juice
- ¼ cup olive oil
- 2 teaspoons sugar
- 1 teaspoon kosher salt

CATFISH TACOS

- 1 cup mayonnaise
- 2 tablespoons honey
- 1 tablespoon fresh lime juice
- 1 tablespoon minced chipotle peppers in adobo sauce
- Vegetable oil, for frying
- 1 cup all-purpose flour
- 1½ teaspoons kosher salt
- 1 teaspoon baking powder
- 1 cup club soda
- 1½ tablespoons hot sauce
- 3 cups panko (Japanese bread crumbs)
- 1½ pounds catfish fillets, cut into 2-inch pieces
- 1 (16-ounce) package flour tortillas

FOR THE APPLE SLAW

In a large bowl, combine slaw mix, apple, carrot, onion, and jalapeño. In a small bowl, whisk together lemon juice, oil, sugar, and salt until smooth. Pour dressing over slaw mixture, tossing to combine. Cover and refrigerate at least 2 hours.

FOR THE CATFISH TACOS

In the work bowl of a food processor, combine mayonnaise, honey, lime juice, and chipotle. Pulse until smooth. Cover, and refrigerate at least 2 hours.

Preheat oven to 200°.

In a large Dutch oven, pour oil to a depth of 4 inches, and heat over medium-high heat until deep-fry thermometer registers 375°.

In a shallow dish, combine flour, salt, and baking powder. Whisk in club soda and hot sauce until smooth. Place bread crumbs in another shallow dish. Dip fish pieces in batter, allowing excess to drip off; coat in bread crumbs. Fry fish, in batches, 1 to 2 minutes per side or until browned. Let drain on paper towels; keep warm in oven.

Spray both sides of tortillas with nonstick cooking spray. In a large skillet over medium heat, cook tortillas 1 to 2 minutes per side or until lightly browned. To assemble tacos, spread tortillas with mayonnaise mixture, and top with fish pieces and Apple Slaw. Serve immediately.

As a mother of four, Joan Chastain knows how to make fresh flavors kids love. When entertaining her kids' friends at her Baton Rouge home, she often whips up big batches of these crunchy catfish tacos.

Louisiana Stir-Fry Shrimp

MAKES 2 SERVINGS

3   tablespoons all-purpose flour
1   teaspoon celery flakes
½   teaspoon Creole seasoning
½   teaspoon garlic powder
½   pound small fresh shrimp, peeled
3½ tablespoons olive oil
1   tablespoon butter
½   cup sliced red onion
1   clove garlic, thinly sliced
5   green onions, chopped (green parts only)
1   stalk celery, chopped
2   mini carrots, julienned
¼   cup seafood or chicken broth
3   cups cooked long-grain rice

Preheat oven to 200°. In a large bowl, combine flour, celery flakes, Creole seasoning, and garlic powder. Add shrimp to flour mixture, and toss to coat.

In a large skillet, heat oil and butter over medium heat. Add red onion and garlic, and cook 2 minutes or until almost brown. Set aside onion mixture in a rimmed baking sheet.

In same skillet, cook shrimp until pink and firm, turning once. Combine shrimp with onion mixture, and place in oven. In same skillet, add green onion, celery, and carrot, and cook about 2 minutes. Deglaze skillet with broth. Add cooked rice to vegetable mixture, and cook until heated through. Divide rice mixture between plates, and top with shrimp mixture.

When home cook Claudius Whitmeyer prepares this quick stir-fry for his family, he often amps up the flavor of the rice by cooking it in equal parts chicken stock and water.

Shrimp Pho

MAKES 6 TO 8 SERVINGS

12 cups water
2 cups chicken broth
Shells from 3 pounds large shrimp
½ bunch fresh cilantro, roughly chopped
1½ cups chopped yellow onion
1⅓ cups chopped green bell pepper
4 cloves garlic, minced
3 tablespoons fish sauce
2 tablespoons fresh lime juice
2 tablespoons soy sauce
1 tablespoon minced fresh ginger
1 teaspoon Sriracha sauce, plus more to taste
½ teaspoon ground coriander
1½ pounds large fresh shrimp, peeled and deveined
1 (8-ounce) package rice noodles
1 to 2 jalapeños, sliced
2 limes, cut into wedges
½ cup Thai basil leaves

In a large stockpot, combine 12 cups water, broth, shells, cilantro, onion, bell pepper, garlic, fish sauce, lime juice, soy sauce, ginger, Sriracha, and coriander. Bring to a boil over medium-high heat; reduce heat, and simmer, uncovered, 1 hour. Strain through a fine-mesh sieve; discard solids. (At this point, pho base can be refrigerated up to 3 days or frozen up to 3 months.)

In a large stockpot, bring pho base to a boil over medium-high heat. Reduce heat to a simmer, and add shrimp and rice noodles. Cook 6 to 8 minutes or until shrimp are pink and firm and noodles are cooked through.

Serve pho topped with sliced jalapeño, lime, and basil. Add additional Sriracha to each serving to taste.

Vietnamese influences have been growing throughout South Louisiana, and on cool days, spicy, brothy pho is one of the most popular dishes around New Orleans.

Baked Whole Fish

1   (4-pound) fish, cleaned with head, fins, and scales removed
½   cup extra-virgin olive oil, divided
2   teaspoons kosher salt
1½   teaspoons ground black pepper
4   cloves garlic, peeled and smashed
3   lemons, sliced and divided
½   cup fresh dill sprigs, divided

Preheat oven to 350°. Coat a large baking dish or roasting pan with cooking spray. Let fish stand at room temperature for 30 minutes.

Score each side of fish 3 times, cutting to the bone. Rub fish with ¼ cup oil, and season with salt and pepper.

Place garlic, half of lemon, and ¼ cup dill inside fish, and transfer to prepared pan. Top fish with remaining lemon and ¼ cup dill. Add remaining ¼ cup oil to pan.

Bake about 45 minutes or until fish flakes from the backbone.

Note: Scoring the fish helps ensure even cooking.

Baked with lemon and garlic, this whole fish from Chef Mark Falgoust is a simply elegant addition to your weeknight table.

When her son played football for Louisiana State University, home cook Charlotte Bollinger made large batches of this chowder to feed the team.

Corn-Bacon-Crab Chowder

MAKES 16 TO 20 SERVINGS

¾ pound bacon
1 cup butter
2 cups all-purpose flour
4 cups chopped yellow onion
½ cup chopped red bell pepper
8 cups warm whole milk (105° to 110°)
8 cups water
3 (15.25-ounce) cans corn
3 (10.75-ounce) cans cream of chicken soup
2 (14.75-ounce) cans cream-style corn
1 (8-ounce) jar Cheddar-flavored cheese dip*
¼ cup Lea and Perrins Marinade for Chicken
¼ cup hot sauce
2 tablespoons chicken bouillon granules
¼ teaspoon garlic powder
¼ teaspoon seasoned salt
2 pounds lump crabmeat, picked free of shell
1 teaspoon ground black pepper
½ teaspoon salt
Garnish: crumbled bacon, chopped red bell pepper

In a large stockpot, cook bacon over medium heat until crisp. Remove bacon from skillet, and let drain on paper towels; reserve 2 tablespoons bacon drippings in stockpot. Crumble bacon when cool. Set aside.

In a large stockpot, heat reserved bacon drippings and butter over medium heat until butter has melted. Stir in flour, and cook 5 minutes, stirring constantly. Stir in onion and bell pepper; reduce heat to low, and cook 15 minutes, stirring often.

Using an immersion blender, blend until smooth. Return to stockpot.

Add reserved bacon, 8 cups water, corn, chicken soup, cream-style corn, cheese dip, marinade, hot sauce, chicken bouillon, garlic powder, and seasoned salt. Bring mixture to a boil over high heat; reduce heat, and simmer 15 minutes. Stir in crab, pepper, and salt. Cook until heated through. Garnish with additional crumbled bacon and bell pepper, if desired.

*We used Cheez Whiz.

Marinated Crab Claws

1 cup olive oil
1 cup tarragon vinegar
¼ cup fresh lemon juice
3 tablespoons chopped fresh shallot
3 tablespoons chopped fresh chives
2 tablespoons crushed red pepper
2 tablespoons chopped fresh parsley
2 tablespoons Cajun seasoning
1 pound crab claws
Lemon wedges

In a medium bowl, whisk together oil, vinegar, lemon juice, shallot, chives, red pepper, parsley, and Cajun seasoning. Set aside ⅓ cup vinaigrette in a small bowl.

In a resealable plastic bag, combine crab claws and remaining marinade. Refrigerate for at least 2 hours before serving.

Remove crab claws from refrigerator 30 minutes before serving, and discard excess marinade. Serve crab claws with lemon wedges and reserved marinade.

Whether you're watching a football game at home or tailgating, these marinated crab claws are perfect for the big game.

Creole Seafood Gumbo

½   cup plus 2 tablespoons unsalted butter, divided
⅓   cup all-purpose flour
¼   cup chopped sweet onion
¼   cup chopped celery
1   teaspoon crushed red pepper
2   cups canned crushed tomatoes
2   teaspoons kosher salt, divided
1   cup seafood stock
2   teaspoons liquid crab boil
2   teaspoons filé powder
2   cloves garlic, minced
1   pound large fresh shrimp, peeled and deveined
1   (8-ounce) container shucked oysters, drained
1   cup dry white wine
Garnish: chopped fresh parsley

In a large Dutch oven, heat ¼ cup butter over medium-high heat; whisk in flour until smooth. Cook, whisking frequently, until roux is light brown. Remove from heat, and set aside.

In a large skillet, melt ¼ cup butter over medium high-heat. Add onion, celery, and pepper, and cook about 3 minutes or until tender. Stir mixture into the roux. Stir tomatoes, 1 teaspoon salt, and seafood stock into roux, and simmer about 15 minutes or until thickened. Stir in crab boil and filé powder.

In a large skillet over medium-high heat, melt remaining 2 tablespoons butter. Add garlic and remaining 1 teaspoon salt, and cook about 30 seconds. Add shrimp, and cook about 2 minutes per side or until just pink; add oysters, and cook about 2 minutes. Add white wine; simmer 2 minutes. Stir seafood mixture into vegetable mixture, and serve immediately. Garnish with fresh parsley, if desired.

*Shrimp, oysters, and tomatoes come together
to give this gumbo a bright, fresh flavor.*

Smoky Crab Dip with Toasted Herbed Baguette Rounds

MAKES 6 TO 8 SERVINGS

BAGUETTE ROUNDS

1   French baguette, sliced into ¼-inch rounds
½   cup butter, melted
2   tablespoons chopped fresh parsley
1   tablespoon chopped fresh chives
½   teaspoon Cajun seasoning

CRAB DIP

2   (8-ounce) packages whipped cream cheese, softened
1   cup plain Greek yogurt
3   tablespoons chopped green onion
2   tablespoons minced shallot
1   tablespoon Worcestershire sauce
1   tablespoon grated fresh horseradish
1   tablespoon Creole seasoning
2   teaspoons fresh lemon juice
2   teaspoons liquid smoke
1   teaspoon minced fresh garlic
1   teaspoon ground black pepper
1   (8-ounce) container crab claw meat, picked free of shell
1   (8-ounce) container lump crabmeat, picked free of shell

FOR THE BAGUETTE ROUNDS
Preheat oven to 350°. Line a baking sheet with foil; set aside.

Lightly brush bread slices with butter. In a small bowl, combine parsley, chives, and Cajun seasoning; sprinkle over bread slices. Bake 12 minutes or until toasted. Remove from oven, and let cool completely.

FOR THE CRAB DIP
In a large bowl, beat cream cheese and yogurt with a mixer at medium-high speed for 2 minutes or until smooth and creamy.

Add onion, shallot, Worcestershire, horseradish, and Creole seasoning. Beat at medium speed until combined. Add lemon juice, liquid smoke, garlic, and pepper, beating until combined. Using a spatula, gently fold crab into mixture.

Serve with Toasted Herbed Baguette Rounds.

Make-ahead dishes like this smoke-infused crab dip are the backbone of a great tailgating spread.

Smothered Okra with Shrimp and Andouille Sausage

MAKES ABOUT 8 SERVINGS

½ cup vegetable oil, divided
1 pound fresh okra, cut into 1-inch pieces
1 cup chopped yellow onion
½ cup chopped red bell pepper
3 tablespoons minced garlic
½ pound andouille sausage, cut into ½-inch pieces
2 (12-ounce) jars roasted red peppers, drained and puréed
2 cups seafood stock
1 (6-ounce) can tomato paste
2 teaspoons kosher salt
1½ teaspoons ground black pepper
½ teaspoon cayenne pepper
1 pound medium fresh shrimp, peeled
3 cups brown jasmine rice, cooked according to package directions*
Garnish: fresh thyme leaves

In a large saucepan, heat ¼ cup oil over medium-high heat. Add okra, and cook 8 to 10 minutes or until tender; remove okra, and set aside.

In the same pan, add remaining ¼ cup oil, and heat over medium-high heat. Add onion, bell pepper, and garlic. Cook, stirring often, 5 to 7 minutes or until tender.

Add sausage, and cook until sausage is browned. Stir in puréed red peppers, stock, tomato paste, salt, pepper, and cayenne. Cook, stirring often, until mixture comes to a boil. Add okra; reduce heat and simmer over medium heat for 20 minutes. Add shrimp, and cook until pink and firm. Serve over rice, and garnish with thyme, if desired.

*We used Cajun Grain Brown Jasmine Rice.

Smoky andouille sausage brings this dish of smothered okra and shrimp together.

Rosemary-Lemon Shrimp Skewers

MAKES 6 SERVINGS

½   cup olive oil
2   tablespoons chopped fresh rosemary
1   tablespoon fresh lemon zest
1½ teaspoons kosher salt
1   teaspoon ground black pepper
1½ pounds extra-jumbo fresh shrimp,
    peeled and deveined (tails left on)
18 (8- to 10-inch) sprigs fresh rosemary,
    soaked in water for 30 minutes
2   lemons, cut into wedges
2   medium zucchini, sliced 2 inches thick

In a small bowl, combine oil, rosemary, lemon zest, salt, and pepper, whisking to combine. Add shrimp, tossing to coat. Cover, and refrigerate 1 hour.

Spray grill rack with nonflammable cooking spray. Preheat grill to medium-high heat (350° to 400°). Strip rosemary leaves from stems, leaving 2 to 3 inches with leaves remaining at the end. Reserve remaining leaves for another use. Thread shrimp onto rosemary sprigs, alternating with lemon and zucchini. Grill skewers uncovered for 2 minutes. Turn skewers, and grill about 2 minutes more or until shrimp are pink and firm.

In these zesty shrimp skewers, the rosemary stalks add an elegant touch and a delicious herbal flavor.

Crawfish Boudin

MAKES ABOUT 1 DOZEN LINKS

2 pounds cooked crawfish tails
1½ teaspoons salt
½ teaspoon cayenne pepper
¼ teaspoon ground white pepper
2 tablespoons canola oil
⅓ cup finely chopped green onion, green parts only
1 cup finely chopped onion
½ cup finely chopped green bell pepper
½ cup finely chopped celery
¼ teaspoon minced garlic
1½ cups long-grain white rice, cooked according to package instructions
2 tablespoons finely chopped parsley
8 ounces prepared hog casings
Garnish: stone-ground mustard

In a large bowl, combine crawfish, salt, and peppers. Set aside.

In a large skillet, heat canola oil over medium heat; add onions, bell pepper, celery, and garlic, and cook about 5 minutes or until softened. Add crawfish mixture, and cook 15 minutes more. Remove from heat, and fold in rice and parsley. Stuff casings while filling is still hot, twisting into 4-inch links.

In a large skillet, add crawfish boudin links, and cover with water. Cook over medium-high heat, keeping just below a simmer; cook 15 to 20 minutes or until heated through. Drain.

In a large skillet, add crawfish boudin, and cook over medium-high heat until golden brown on all sides. Serve immediately with mustard, if desired.

While it isn't the pork-liver-based boudin that is famous across much of Louisiana, this crawfish boudin from writer Jay D. Ducote packs its own punch of flavor that can be enjoyed smoked, pan seared, or deep fried in the form of crawfish boudin balls.

Shrimp Bisque

MAKES 6 TO 8 SERVINGS

½ cup butter
¾ cup all-purpose flour
½ cup chopped yellow onion
¼ cup chopped celery
¼ cup chopped green bell pepper
2 cloves garlic, minced
½ teaspoon Old Bay Seasoning
2 cups half-and-half
8½ cups Shrimp Stock (page 156)
¼ cup brandy
5 tablespoons tomato paste
1 teaspoon smoked paprika
1 pound large fresh shrimp, peeled and deveined
Garnish: dry sherry, chopped fresh parsley
French bread

In a large Dutch oven, melt butter over medium heat. Add flour, and cook, stirring constantly, 6 minutes. Stir in onion, celery, bell pepper, garlic, and Old Bay. Cook, stirring constantly, 7 minutes. Add half-and-half. With an immersion blender, blend until smooth.

Add Shrimp Stock, brandy, tomato paste, and paprika. Bring to a boil over medium-high heat; reduce heat and simmer 35 to 40 minutes. Add shrimp, and cook 8 to 10 minutes or until shrimp are pink and firm. Garnish with a drizzle of sherry and parsley, if desired. Serve with French bread.

Starting off with a blond roux and sizzling trinity, this comforting shrimp bisque will brighten any day.

Spaghetti Squash Shrimp Scampi

MAKES 6 SERVINGS

2   (3- to 3½-pound) spaghetti squashes
8   tablespoons butter, divided
1½ pounds large fresh shrimp, peeled and deveined
2   large shallots, minced
3   cloves garlic, minced
1   cup dry white wine
½   cup chicken broth
½   cup heavy whipping cream
2   tablespoons capers
1   teaspoon Creole seasoning
¼   teaspoon crushed red pepper
¼   cup chopped fresh parsley

Preheat oven to 375°. Line a baking sheet with foil.

Using a fork, pierce squashes all over. Place on prepared baking sheet, and roast 1 hour and 20 minutes or until tender. Let cool 15 minutes. Slice in half lengthwise, and shred squash meat with a fork; discard seeds and skin.

In a large skillet, melt 1 tablespoon butter over medium-high heat. Add shrimp, and cook about 5 minutes, turning occasionally, or until pink and firm. Remove shrimp, and set aside.

Melt 1 tablespoon butter in skillet over medium-high heat. Add shallot and garlic; cook, stirring occasionally, 6 minutes. Add wine and broth, increase heat to high, and reduce liquid by two-thirds. Reduce heat to medium-low. Stir in remaining 6 tablespoons butter, cream, capers, Creole seasoning, and red pepper. Cook 3 minutes or until butter has melted and sauce is smooth. Stir in squash, shrimp, and parsley. Serve immediately.

Creamy and full of flavor, this non-traditional shrimp scampi is one of our favorite autumn meals.

HOLIDAY FÊTES

With gatherings around every corner,
we pull out all the stops during the holiday season
with big, bold flavors and traditional dishes.

Catahoula Court-Bouillon

MAKES 8 SERVINGS

⅔ cup vegetable oil
⅔ cup all-purpose flour
2 cups chopped onion
1 cup chopped green bell pepper
½ cup chopped celery
1 teaspoon minced garlic
2 cups diced tomatoes
1 (10-ounce) can diced tomatoes
  with chiles
4 cups fish stock or water
1 tablespoon salt
1 teaspoon cayenne pepper
2½ pounds redfish fillets, skin and bones
  removed, cut into 2-inch pieces
¼ cup chopped green onion
¼ cup finely chopped fresh parsley
3 cups long grain rice, cooked according
  to package directions
1 (16-ounce) loaf French bread, sliced
Hot sauce, for serving

In a large Dutch oven, heat oil over medium heat; whisk in flour until smooth. Cook, whisking frequently, until roux is chocolate-colored. Stir in onion, bell pepper, celery, and garlic; cook 5 minutes or until softened. Stir in tomatoes. Reduce heat to medium-low, and cook, stirring occasionally, 30 minutes or until a paper-like film forms on top.

Add fish stock or water, salt, and cayenne; cook, stirring occasionally, for 1 hour or until mixture has thickened.

Add fish; cover, and cook about 15 minutes or until fish flakes easily with a fork. Stir in green onion and parsley. Serve over rice with French bread and hot sauce, if desired.

A traditional French court-bouillon is a mildly seasoned liquid used to poach fish and seafood. In Louisiana, court-bouillon evolved over time to become a thick and hearty roux-based stew, like this one from writer and chef Marcelle Bienvenu.

Salt-Roasted Shrimp

MAKES ABOUT 4 SERVINGS

3 cups kosher salt
2 pounds unpeeled large fresh shrimp
   (heads left on)
Lemon wedges

Preheat oven to 400°.

On a large rimmed baking sheet, add salt in an even layer. Bake 10 minutes. Remove ½ cup salt and reserve. Arrange shrimp evenly over hot salt; top with ½ cup reserved hot salt. Cover tightly with foil.

Bake 6 to 8 minutes or just until shrimp turn pink. Discard excess salt. Place shrimp on a serving platter; squeeze lemon over shrimp.

Salt-roasting whole shrimp is a great way to ensure a flavorful and tender result.

Crabmeat Ravigote

MAKES 8 TO 10 SERVINGS

⅔ cup mayonnaise
1 tablespoon Dijon mustard
1 tablespoon finely chopped green onion
¼ teaspoon ground black pepper
⅛ teaspoon salt
2 pounds lump crabmeat, picked free of shell
¼ cup capers
1 tablespoon chopped fresh parsley
Belgian endive
Toasted French bread slices
Garnish: capers

In a large bowl, combine mayonnaise, mustard, onion, pepper, and salt. Gently fold in crab and capers until evenly coated. Top with parsley, and serve with endive and French bread. Garnish with capers, if desired.

Quick, easy, and elegant, this crabmeat ravigote from Lockport, Louisiana, home cook Charlotte Bollinger is one of South Louisiana's simple pleasures.

Blue Crab and Corn Soup

MAKES ABOUT 6 SERVINGS

½ cup butter
3 tablespoons corn flour
1 cup chopped onion
¼ cup chopped green onion
2 tablespoons chopped jalapeño
4 cups half-and-half
1 cup chicken broth
2 (15-ounce) cans cream-style corn
3 cups fresh corn kernels
1 (10.75-ounce) can cream of chicken soup
1 teaspoon Creole seasoning
1 teaspoon cayenne pepper
½ teaspoon ground black pepper
1 (8-ounce) container jumbo lump crabmeat, picked free of shell, divided
Garnish: chopped green onion

In a large saucepan, melt butter over medium heat; whisk in corn flour until smooth. Cook, whisking frequently, until roux is tan. Add onions and jalapeño, and cook 10 minutes or until tender. Add half-and-half, broth, corn, soup, Creole seasoning, cayenne, and black pepper, stirring to combine. Cook 20 minutes.

Add half of crabmeat to soup; cook 10 minutes. Stir in remaining crabmeat before serving, and garnish with chopped green onion, if desired. Store covered in refrigerator for up to 3 days.

Creamy and studded with luscious lumps of crabmeat, this soup is an ideal addition to your holiday table.

Holiday Bouillabaisse

MAKES 4 TO 6 SERVINGS

1 pound redfish fillets, skin removed*
1 pound drum fillets, skin removed*
3 teaspoons salt, divided
1½ teaspoons cayenne pepper, divided
1 (28-ounce) can whole tomatoes
3 cups chopped yellow onion
2 cups chopped green bell pepper
1 cup chopped celery
3 cloves garlic, minced
1 tablespoon chopped fresh thyme
½ cup unsalted butter
4 bay leaves
1 lemon, sliced
2 cups fish stock
½ cup white wine
1 pound medium fresh shrimp, peeled and deveined
1 pound lump crabmeat, picked free of shell
24 oysters, shucked and drained
Sliced toasted French bread
Garnish: chopped fresh parsley

Season fish with 2 teaspoons salt and ½ teaspoon cayenne. In a medium bowl, add tomatoes and juice, and mash until small chunks remain. In another medium bowl, combine onion, bell pepper, celery, garlic, thyme, remaining 1 teaspoon salt, and remaining 1 teaspoon cayenne.

In a large Dutch oven, melt butter over medium heat. Add onion mixture, and cook 6 to 8 minutes or until softened. Add tomato, bay leaves, lemon, stock, and wine. Bring to a boil over high heat; reduce heat, and simmer; add fish. Cover, and cook 45 minutes. Do not stir.

Gently stir in shrimp, crabmeat, and oysters, making sure to fully submerge, and simmer 12 minutes. Place a toasted bread slice in each bowl, and ladle soup over. Garnish with parsley, if desired.

*Red snapper and halibut fillets may be substituted.

Mix and match seasonal fish fillets in this decadent holiday stew. The exact amounts of each can vary according to taste and availability, provided the total yield is the same.

Gulf Shrimp and Littleneck Clams with Chorizo and Tomato-Fennel Broth

MAKES 4 SERVINGS

TOMATO-FENNEL BROTH

2   tablespoons olive oil
2   cups chopped fennel
1   cup chopped onion
1   cup chopped celery
4   cloves garlic, sliced
1   (32-ounce) can whole San Marzano
    tomatoes, chopped
½   cup white wine
6   cups shrimp or chicken stock
1   teaspoon sea salt
1   teaspoon ground fennel seed
¼   teaspoon ground black pepper
⅛   teaspoon crushed red pepper

SHRIMP AND CHORIZO

1   cup dried cannellini beans, soaked
    at least 8 hours
1   tablespoon salt, plus more to taste
1   dried bay leaf
3   tablespoons extra-virgin olive oil,
    divided
12 ounces dry Spanish chorizo, sliced
24 littleneck clams, washed
4   cups Tomato-Fennel Broth
1   pound large fresh shrimp, peeled
    and deveined
Ground black pepper to taste
Garnish: chopped chives or fennel fronds

FOR THE TOMATO-FENNEL BROTH

In a stockpot, heat oil over medium heat. Add fennel, onion, celery, and garlic, and cook, stirring occasionally, for 12 to 15 minutes or until vegetables are softened. Add tomato, and cook 10 minutes more. Add wine, and cook 5 minutes more. Add stock, salt, fennel seed, and peppers; simmer for 30 minutes. Set aside 4 cups Tomato-Fennel Broth, and reserve remaining Tomato-Fennel Broth for another use.

FOR THE SHRIMP AND CHORIZO

In a small saucepan, add beans and cover with water; add salt and bay leaf. Bring to a boil; reduce heat; and simmer 20 minutes or until tender. Remove from heat; drain, and reserve beans.

In a stockpot, heat 2 tablespoons oil over medium-high heat. Pat chorizo with paper towels to remove excess oil. Add chorizo, and cook for 2 minutes. Add clams, and cook 2 minutes more. Add 4 cups Tomato-Fennel Broth; simmer 4 to 5 minutes or until clams just start to open.

Add shrimp and beans, and cook 2 to 3 minutes or just until shrimp turn pink and firm. Season broth to taste with salt and pepper. Divide mixture among four large bowls; drizzle with remaining 1 tablespoon oil, and garnish with chives if desired.

New Orleans chef Alex Harrell combines Spanish influences with Louisiana shrimp for this flavorful, brothy dish.

Broiled Oysters with Spinach and Andouille

MAKES ABOUT 8 SERVINGS

1   (9-ounce) bag fresh spinach
3   tablespoons butter, divided
1   cup finely chopped onion
¼   cup finely chopped celery
¼   pound fresh andouille sausage, casings removed
3   cloves garlic, minced
2   tablespoons white wine
½   cup clam juice
½   teaspoon salt
½   cup panko (Japanese bread crumbs)
2   dozen fresh oysters on the half shell

Bring a large Dutch oven of salted water to a boil. Add spinach, and stir about 1 minute or until just wilted. Drain, reserving ½ cup cooking liquid, and squeeze dry. Chop, and set aside.

In a medium skillet, melt 1 tablespoon butter over medium heat. Add onion and celery, and cook 3 minutes or until browned. Add sausage, and cook 15 minutes or until browned, stirring to crumble.

Add garlic, and cook 2 minutes. Add white wine, and scrape any browned bits from bottom of pan. Continue cooking 30 seconds or until wine evaporates. Add spinach, ½ cup reserved cooking liquid, clam juice, and salt; simmer 15 minutes or until liquid is almost evaporated. Remove from heat; stir in remaining 2 tablespoons butter and bread crumbs.

Preheat oven to broil. Position oven rack 6 inches from broiler. Line a large rimmed baking sheet with foil.

Run a knife under meat of oyster to release from shells. Arrange shell bottoms (containing oysters) on prepared pan. Top each oyster with about 1 tablespoon sausage mixture. Broil 5 minutes or until lightly browned.

New Orleans home entertainer Sarah Landrum prepares these broiled oysters each Christmas as a part of her family's Réveillon dinner.

For a lighter version of this wintertime favorite, author Holly Clegg relies on classic Louisiana herbs and spices.

Oyster Artichoke Soup

MAKES 6 SERVINGS

2 tablespoons olive oil
1 bunch green onions, chopped
1 teaspoon minced garlic
¼ cup all-purpose flour
1½ cups fat-free chicken broth
1 pint oysters, drained, ½ cup liquid reserved
1 bay leaf
½ teaspoon fresh thyme leaves
Dash cayenne pepper
2 (14-ounce) cans artichoke hearts, drained and coarsely chopped
¼ cup chopped parsley
1 cup fat-free half-and-half
¼ cup sherry
Garnish: fresh thyme leaves

In a medium nonstick saucepan, heat olive oil over medium heat; add green onion and garlic, and cook 5 minutes. Add flour, stirring constantly, until combined. Gradually add chicken broth and oyster liquid. Add bay leaf, thyme, and cayenne.

Bring to boil; reduce heat, and simmer about 15 minutes. Add oysters, artichokes, and parsley; cook 10 minutes or until oysters curl around edges.

Stir in half-and-half and sherry, and cook until thoroughly heated. Discard bay leaf before serving. Garnish with fresh thyme leaves, if desired.

Papa's Bouillabaisse

MAKES 8 SERVINGS

ROUILLE

¾ cup mayonnaise
2 tablespoons minced garlic
1 teaspoon chopped fresh parsley
1 teaspoon fresh lemon juice
½ teaspoon salt
¼ teaspoon ground black pepper

BOUILLABAISSE

2½ pounds redfish fillets, skin and bones removed*
3 teaspoons salt, divided
1 teaspoon cayenne pepper, divided
1 (28-ounce) can whole tomatoes
3 cups coarsely chopped yellow onion
2 cups coarsely chopped green bell pepper
2 stalks celery, coarsely chopped
3 cloves garlic, minced
½ cup butter
1 pound medium fresh shrimp, peeled and deveined
1 pound lump crabmeat, picked free of shell
4 bay leaves
⅓ cup dry white wine
1 (16-ounce) loaf French bread, sliced and toasted

FOR THE ROUILLE
In a small bowl, combine all ingredients. Cover and refrigerate.

FOR THE BOUILLABAISSE
Season fish fillets with 2 teaspoons salt and ½ teaspoon cayenne. In a medium bowl, mash tomatoes in juice until only small pieces remain. In another medium bowl, combine onion, bell pepper, celery, garlic, remaining 1 teaspoon salt, and remaining ½ teaspoon cayenne.

In a large Dutch oven, melt butter over medium heat. Place 2 fish fillets in bottom of pot. Top fish with one-third each of tomatoes and vegetable mixture. Repeat layers until all fish, tomatoes, and vegetables are used. Top with shrimp, crabmeat, and bay leaves. Pour wine over, and bring to a boil. Reduce heat to a low simmer; cover pot, and cook for 1 hour. Do not stir.

Place a toasted bread slice in each of 8 bowls, and ladle soup over. Spread remaining bread slices with Rouille, and serve with soup.

*Red snapper, black drum, speckled trout, or any firm-fleshed fish may be substituted for redfish.

After a day of fishing near her family's Atchafalaya fish camp, writer and chef Marcelle Bienvenu often makes this savory stew.

Oyster Pan Roast

MAKES ABOUT 4 SERVINGS

4   slices bacon
1   fennel bulb, trimmed, quartered, and thinly sliced
¾   teaspoon plus ⅛ teaspoon salt, divided
½   teaspoon plus ⅛ teaspoon ground black pepper, divided
1   cup julienned oyster mushroom caps (about 3 ounces)
¼   cup diced shallot
1   pint oysters, drained, ½ cup liquid reserved
1½   cups heavy whipping cream
½   cup Yukon gold potatoes, diced medium and cooked in salted water until just tender
½   teaspoon chopped fresh thyme
1   tablespoon chopped parsley
1   tablespoon chopped fennel fronds
4   slices grilled ciabatta

In a medium skillet over medium-high heat, add bacon, and cook until crispy. Set aside, and crumble when cool; reserve 3 tablespoons bacon drippings.

In a large bowl, combine fennel, ½ teaspoon salt, and ¼ teaspoon pepper. In same skillet over medium heat, add 1 tablespoon reserved bacon drippings. Add fennel, and cook, stirring occasionally, until caramelized. Set aside.

In same skillet over medium-high heat, add remaining 2 tablespoons reserved bacon drippings. Add mushrooms, and cook 3 to 4 minutes or until crispy; reduce heat if pan begins to smoke. Add ⅛ teaspoon salt and ⅛ teaspoon pepper, stirring to combine. Using a slotted spoon, remove mushrooms, and let drain on paper towels. Return skillet to heat; reduce heat to medium.

Add shallot, and cook until tender. If mixture looks dry, add 1 to 2 tablespoons oil. Add oyster liquor, and reduce by half. Add cream, and reduce by half. The mixture should just coat the back of a wooden spoon.

Add potatoes, reserved fennel and bacon, thyme, parsley, fennel fronds, and oysters to pan. Cook over medium heat until oyster edges just begin to curl. Add reserved mushrooms, remaining ¼ teaspoon salt, and remaining ¼ teaspoon pepper. Place ciabatta slices in 4 bowls, and top with oyster mixture.

On chilly New Orleans winter days, chef Kristen Essig serves this creamy, comforting oyster pan roast.

Shrimp Ya-Ya

MAKES 4 SERVINGS

QUICK ALFREDO SAUCE

1   tablespoon butter
¼   cup heavy whipping cream
6   tablespoons grated Parmesan cheese
¾   teaspoon minced garlic
½   teaspoon chopped fresh parsley
⅛   teaspoon crushed red pepper (optional)

SHRIMP YA-YA

2   cups fresh basil leaves
2   tablespoons pine nuts
1   clove garlic
3   tablespoons olive oil, divided
¼   cup plus 2 tablespoons grated Parmesan cheese, divided
½   teaspoon kosher salt
1   pound extra jumbo shrimp, peeled and deveined
2   teaspoons crushed red pepper

FOR THE QUICK ALFREDO SAUCE
In a medium saucepan, melt butter over medium heat. Add cream, and simmer for 5 minutes. Add Parmesan and garlic, stirring until cheese melts. Remove from heat, and let thicken. Add parsley and red pepper, if desired.

FOR THE SHRIMP YA-YA
In the work bowl of a food processer, add basil, pine nuts, and garlic, and pulse to combine. With motor running, add 2 tablespoons oil in a steady stream, and process until a smooth paste forms. Add 2 tablespoons Parmesan and salt, and process 30 seconds more.

In a large nonstick skillet, heat remaining 1 tablespoon oil over medium-high heat. Add shrimp, and cook until pink and firm; stir in red pepper, basil mixture, and Quick Alfredo Sauce. Cook until sauce is slightly thickened. Top with remaining ¼ cup Parmesan.

Cheesy, creamy, and full of flavor, this Shrimp Ya-Ya from Chef Chris Hayes is just about the ultimate crowd-pleaser.

Creamy Smoked Sweet Potato Soup

MAKES 6 TO 8 SERVINGS

Pecan wood chips soaked in water
    at least 30 minutes
4   extra-large sweet potatoes
    (about 5 pounds)
4   cups seafood stock
2   cups heavy whipping cream
¾   teaspoon kosher salt, divided
½   teaspoon ground cinnamon
¼   teaspoon ground nutmeg
1   pound fresh jumbo lump crabmeat,
    picked free of shell
1   tablespoon fresh lemon juice
⅛   teaspoon crushed red pepper
2   tablespoons unsalted butter, melted
1   tablespoon thinly sliced chives

Preheat smoker to 200° to 225°. Sprinkle wood chips over coals.

Smoke sweet potatoes on a rimmed baking sheet 2½ to 3 hours. Let cool; peel, and roughly chop. In a large Dutch oven, combine sweet potato, stock, and cream. With an immersion blender, blend on high speed until smooth. Heat over medium heat, and add ½ teaspoon salt, cinnamon, and nutmeg. Strain mixture through a fine-mesh sieve into a large bowl.

In a medium bowl, combine crab, lemon juice, red pepper, remaining ¼ teaspoon salt, butter, and chives. Divide soup among bowls, and top with crabmeat mixture.

In this autumnal showstopper of a soup, New Orleans home cook Samantha Foglesong combines sweet crabmeat with smoked sweet potatoes.

Oyster Roast

MAKES 6 TO 8 SERVINGS

SPICY COCKTAIL SAUCE

½   cup ketchup
¼   cup hot sauce
2   tablespoons prepared horseradish, drained
1   teaspoon fresh lemon juice
1   teaspoon chopped fresh parsley

GARLIC-BUTTER SAUCE

½   cup unsalted butter
2   cloves garlic, minced
2   tablespoons chopped shallot
1   tablespoon fresh lemon juice
1   teaspoon kosher salt
1   teaspoon chopped fresh thyme

TARRAGON-BLACK PEPPER SAUCE

⅓   cup mayonnaise
¼   cup sour cream
2   tablespoons white wine vinegar
1   tablespoon chopped fresh tarragon
1   teaspoon kosher salt
1   teaspoon ground black pepper

OYSTER ROAST

8   lemons, halved
8   dozen fresh oysters

FOR THE SPICY COCKTAIL SAUCE
In a small bowl, combine all ingredients. Cover and refrigerate up to 1 week.

FOR THE GARLIC-BUTTER SAUCE
In a small saucepan, melt butter over medium heat; stir in garlic and shallot. Cook about 1 minute or until soft and translucent; stir in lemon juice, salt, and thyme. Keep warm until serving, or cover and refrigerate up to 3 days. Warm before serving.

FOR THE TARRAGON-BLACK PEPPER SAUCE
In a small bowl, combine all ingredients. Cover and refrigerate up to 3 days.

FOR THE OYSTER ROAST
Preheat grill to high heat (400° to 450°).

Place lemons, cut side down, on grill, and grill 2 minutes or until browned.

Place oysters on grill, and grill 10 minutes or until the shells barely open. Remove from grill; shuck using a towel or silicon oven mitt. (Oysters will be very hot.) Serve with Spicy Cocktail Sauce, Garlic-Butter Sauce, Tarragon-Black Pepper Sauce, and grilled lemons, if desired.

Hosting a backyard oyster roast is a lovely way to enjoy a fall or early winter afternoon.

Basics
ROUX

A ROUX IS A MIXTURE of flour and fat (vegetable oil and butter are the most common) that acts as a thickener and flavoring agent in many Cajun and Creole dishes. This single element can range from the nearly flavorless white roux to the complex, nutty chocolate roux many cooks prefer.

Though it only requires two ingredients, don't underestimate a roux, not even for a second. The stovetop method takes constant stirring and loving attention for up to 45 minutes. A burned roux, which turns black and has grains resembling coffee grounds, can ruin an otherwise excellent gumbo.

Thankfully, there's more than one way to make a roux, including a low-maintenance oven method and even one for the microwave. No matter how you prepare your roux, remember that all that careful, patient stirring will help make an unforgettable meal.

STOVETOP ROUX
MAKES ABOUT 1 CUP

7 tablespoons vegetable oil or butter
11 tablespoons all-purpose flour

1. In a large cast-iron skillet, heat oil over medium-high heat; whisk in flour until smooth. Cook, whisking frequently, 4 to 5 minutes or until flour has lost its raw smell. Continue cooking, whisking frequently, until desired color forms. A dark brown roux can take about 45 minutes to form.
2. Remove from heat, and use immediately, or let cool, and freeze up to 6 months.

OVEN ROUX
MAKES ABOUT 4 CUPS

2 cups vegetable oil or butter
2 cups all-purpose flour

1. Preheat oven to 350°.
2. In a large cast-iron or ovenproof skillet, combine oil and flour. Whisk until smooth. Bake roux, stirring every 20 minutes, for about 2 hours or until a blond roux forms. Continue cooking, stirring every 5 minutes, until desired color is reached.

MICROWAVE ROUX
MAKES ABOUT 2 CUPS

1 cup vegetable oil or butter
1 cup all-purpose flour

1. In a 4-cup glass measuring cup, combine oil and flour, and whisk until smooth.
2. Microwave mixture, uncovered, on high about 5 minutes or until a blond roux forms. Carefully remove from microwave, and stir with a wooden spoon until smooth. Continue cooking in 1- to 2-minute intervals or until desired color forms, stirring between each.

Dry Roux

Make a "dry roux" by baking all-purpose flour on a rimmed baking sheet at 400° until desired color forms. Substitute same amount of dry roux for flour in recipe, and whisk into hot oil until smooth.

Roux Tips

As roux darkens, stir it more frequently.
Try other fats. (Duck fat roux is divine.)
Prepared roux can be frozen up to 6 months.

TRINITY

IF ROUX IS THE BASE of many Cajun dishes—especially gumbos and étouffées—then the trinity is certainly right behind it. This time-honored combination of finely chopped onion, bell pepper, and celery adds to the flavor of the roux and builds on its dark, roasty foundation.

Culinary traditions around the world each have their own set of distinct flavors and techniques, and it makes sense that the trinity would find its home in Acadiana. As a largely Spanish and French cultural mash-up, the Cajun trinity bears a resemblance to French mirepoix and Spanish sofrito.

And as with a roux, there is no one "right" way to prepare the trinity. Think of the traditional trinity as a springboard to other flavorful combinations. To start you off, we came up with a couple of variations, including one smoky and another full of spice.

TRADITIONAL TRINITY
MAKES 2 CUPS

1   cup finely chopped onion
½   cup finely chopped green bell pepper
½   cup finely chopped celery

1. In a small bowl, combine all ingredients. Use immediately, or cover, and refrigerate up to 3 days.

SMOKY TRINITY
MAKES ABOUT 2 CUPS

1   poblano pepper, halved and seeded
1   cup finely chopped onion
½   cup finely chopped celery
3   cloves garlic, minced
2   teaspoons smoked paprika
1   teaspoon ground chipotle chile pepper
1   teaspoon salt
½   teaspoon ground black pepper

1. Preheat oven to 450°. Line a baking sheet with foil. Place pepper halves, skin side up, on prepared pan. Bake for 30 minutes or until skin is blackened.

2. Place pepper in a resealable plastic bag (or in a bowl, and cover with plastic wrap). Let stand for 15 minutes or until cool enough to handle. Peel peppers, discarding skin. Chop pepper, and transfer to a small bowl. Add onion, celery, garlic, paprika, chipotle, salt, and black pepper. Use immediately, or cover, and refrigerate up to 3 days.

SPICY TRINITY
MAKES ABOUT 1¾ CUPS

1   cup finely chopped onion
½   cup finely chopped celery
¼   cup finely chopped jalapeño
3   cloves garlic, minced
2   teaspoons crushed red pepper
1   teaspoon cayenne pepper
1   teaspoon salt
½   teaspoon ground black pepper

1. In a small bowl, combine all ingredients. Use immediately, or cover, and refrigerate up to 3 days.

TRINITY
3 WAYS

Basics

SPICE BLENDS

Building layers of flavor is a central idea of Louisiana cooking, and spice mixes are an essential element in that process. Experiment with these basic mixes until they suit your tastes.

CLASSIC CAJUN SEASONING
MAKES ABOUT ¾ CUP

2	tablespoons garlic powder
2	tablespoons onion powder
2	tablespoons salt
4	teaspoons Hungarian paprika
2	teaspoons ground black pepper
2	teaspoons ground oregano
2	teaspoons ground thyme
1	teaspoon ground cumin
½	teaspoon dry mustard
½	teaspoon ground celery seed
½	teaspoon ground chipotle chile pepper

1. In a small bowl, combine all ingredients. Transfer to a sealed container, and store up to 6 months.

EXTRA-SPICY CAJUN SEASONING
MAKES ABOUT 1 CUP

2	tablespoons garlic powder
2	tablespoons onion powder
2	tablespoons salt
4	teaspoons chili powder
2	teaspoons Hungarian paprika
2	teaspoons ground black pepper
2	teaspoons ground dried green bell pepper
2	teaspoons ground dried red bell pepper
2	teaspoons ground jalapeño
2	teaspoons cayenne pepper
2	teaspoons ground chipotle chile pepper
2	teaspoons ground oregano
2	teaspoons ground thyme
1	teaspoon ground cumin
½	teaspoon dry mustard
½	teaspoon ground celery seed

1. In a small bowl, combine all ingredients. Transfer to a sealed container, and store up to 6 months.

SWEET AND SMOKY CAJUN SEASONING
MAKES ABOUT ¾ CUP

2	tablespoons garlic powder
2	tablespoons onion powder
2	tablespoons salt
4	teaspoons smoked paprika
2	teaspoons ground black pepper
2	teaspoons ground Aleppo pepper
2	teaspoons ground dried green bell pepper
2	teaspoons ground dried red bell pepper
2	teaspoons ground oregano
2	teaspoons ground thyme
1	teaspoon ground cumin
½	teaspoon dry mustard
½	teaspoon mace
½	teaspoon ground celery seed
½	teaspoon ground chipotle chile pepper
¼	teaspoon ground cardamom

1. In a small bowl, combine all ingredients. Transfer to a sealed container, and store up to 6 months.

CRAWFISH BOIL PACKET
MAKES 1 PACKET

	Cheesecloth
10	dried bay leaves
1	bunch fresh thyme
¼	cup coriander seeds
¼	cup dill seeds
¼	cup yellow mustard seeds
2	tablespoons cayenne pepper

1. In the center of a double layer of cheesecloth, combine all ingredients. Fold over to make a packet, and tie with butcher's twine.

CRAB BOIL PACKET
MAKES 1 PACKET

	Cheesecloth
¼	cup yellow mustard seeds
3	tablespoons coriander seeds
2	tablespoons sea salt
2	tablespoons chopped fresh dill
2	tablespoons whole allspice
1	tablespoon crushed red pepper
1	tablespoon black peppercorns
1	teaspoon cayenne pepper

1. In the center of a double layer of cheesecloth, combine all ingredients. Fold over to make a packet, and tie with butcher's twine.

Spicy Tip

One of the benefits of using your own seasoning blend is that you can control the amount of salt. Many cooks omit salt from the mix and add to taste when cooking.

SAUCES & STOCKS

ZESTY RÉMOULADE
MAKES ABOUT 1½ CUPS

1	cup mayonnaise
2	tablespoons chopped capers
2	tablespoons chopped cornichons
1	tablespoon chopped fresh parsley
1	teaspoon lemon zest
1	tablespoon fresh lemon juice
1	teaspoon ground paprika
¼	teaspoon cayenne pepper
1	teaspoon salt
½	teaspoon ground black pepper
1	teaspoon Tabasco sauce

1. In a small bowl, whisk together all ingredients until combined. Cover and refrigerate until serving.

SHRIMP STOCK
MAKES ABOUT 8½ CUPS

10	cups water
	Shells from 5 pounds shrimp
¾	cup chopped yellow onion
⅓	cup chopped celery
⅓	cup chopped green bell pepper
⅓	cup dry white wine (optional)
¼	cup chopped parsley leaves and stems
2	teaspoons whole black peppercorns
1	teaspoon Old Bay Seasoning

1. In a stockpot, combine all ingredients. Bring to a boil over medium-high heat; reduce heat and simmer, uncovered, 1 hour. Strain through a fine-mesh sieve, discarding solids. Refrigerate up to 3 days, or freeze up to 3 months.

Note: Save shrimp shells in your freezer until you have enough for stock.

CREOLE BEURRE BLANC
MAKES ABOUT 1 CUP

3	tablespoons minced shallot
2	tablespoons minced green bell pepper
1	tablespoon minced garlic
¾	cup white wine
⅓	cup fresh lemon juice
¼	cup white wine vinegar
2	tablespoons heavy whipping cream
¾	cup cold butter, cut into tablespoons
½	teaspoon Creole seasoning
¼	teaspoon ground black pepper
⅛	teaspoon cayenne pepper

1. In a small nonreactive saucepan, combine shallot, bell pepper, garlic, wine, lemon juice, and vinegar. Cook mixture over high heat about 10 minutes or until reduced to 2 tablespoons. Remove from heat; strain mixture through a fine-mesh sieve, discarding solids. Return liquid to pan, and return pan to heat.
2. Add cream, and whisk constantly until mixture begins to boil; reduce heat to low. Add butter, 1 tablespoon at a time, whisking after each addition until almost melted before adding more. Continue until only 2 to 3 tablespoons butter remain. Remove mixture from heat, and whisk in remaining butter for 1 to 2 minutes until melted. Sauce should be thick and smooth. Add Creole seasoning and peppers. Serve immediately.

CHIMICHURRI SAUCE
MAKES ABOUT 2 CUPS

1	cup fresh parsley
¼	cup chopped green onion
¼	cup fresh cilantro
¼	cup fresh rosemary
¼	cup fresh sage
¼	cup anchovies
¼	cup fresh lemon juice
8	cloves garlic
1	teaspoon salt
2	cups extra-virgin olive oil

1. In the container of a blender, combine all ingredients; process until combined. Transfer to a medium bowl; cover and refrigerate until using. Sauce can be made and frozen up to 1 month in advance.

While store-bought stocks and sauces are a convenient way to shorten cooking times, homemade versions add a brilliant flourish to a memorable meal.

INDEX